Don't Get
Scrooged

How to Thrive
in a World Full of
Obnoxious, Incompetent,
Arrogant, and Downright
Mean-Spirited People

Richard Carlson

HarperSanFrancisco
A Division of HarperCollins*Publishers*

FIRST EDITION

LIBRARY OF CONGRESS CATALOGING-IN-PUBLICATION DATA
Carlson, Richard
Don't get scrooged : how to thrive in a world full of obnoxious, incompetent, arrogant, and downright mean-spirited people / Richard Carlson. — 1st ed.
p. cm.
ISBN–10: 0-06-0758929
ISBN–13: 978-0-06-0758929
1. Interpersonal conflict—Miscellanea. I. Title.
BF637.I48C37   2006
158.2—dc22   2006041231

06 07 08 09 10 RRD(H) 10 9 8 7 6 5 4 3 2 1

Acknowledgments

I dedicate this book to my wife Kris,
and my two daughters Jazzy and Kenna.
Thank you for helping me to feel like the
luckiest man alive. I love you!

I'd like to acknowledge and thank the following people for their invaluable help in the creation of this book:

First, to Gideon Weil and Cynthia DiTiberio, two very intuitive, creative, and talented editors, without whom this book would not be the same! To Linda Chester and Linda Michaels, my literary agents and close friends whom I treasure and thank. To Kris, Jazzy ,and Kenna Carlson, for always being so supportive and patient when I write a book, including this one—I love you all so much. To Susan Miller for your support, integrity, and friendship. Thank you so much for helping me create the time and space to write this book. To Carol Hansen Grey and Victor Grey for your brilliant Web support. To the entire staff at HarperSanFrancisco.Thank you for supporting this idea and helping to make it a reality. To Ken Bradford, whose wisdom and insights help me stay centered while I work; and to my dear friend, John Welshons who helped me with many ideas, kept me laughing, and freely shared his wisdom. Finally, thank you to the hundreds of people who I met, talked to, and learned from over the years. Once again, thank you all so much, for your kindness, love, friendship, and generosity while this book was in progress.

Contents

Introduction

Tis the season ... and items on your to-do list are multiplying daily: trees to trim, cookies to bake, gifts to buy (and wrap, and mail, and deliver), people to see, places to be, pounds to gain. Whether you're driving or flying, going to the office party or hosting one of your own, entering the mall (again) or feeling mauled by traffic, you are not alone. Everyone it seems is doing the same things you are, exponentially upping your odds of not just getting jostled but getting scrooged.

It's as though we are all being dogged by descendants of Ebenezer Scrooge, Charles Dickens's *Christmas Carol* character who left everyone he encountered—at work, on the street, in his family—with something to grumble about.

Not that having a bone to pick with humanity is a purely seasonal ritual. Any day of the year can be—and sometimes is—just a bad day.

As I drove to my office today to write this introduction, I stopped as usual at my favorite coffee shop for my favorite coffee drink. While waiting in line, I overheard three separate conversations, all of which featured people complaining about other people in their lives who were, in one way or another, driving them crazy. Last night, as I was flying home from a trip, everyone around me seemed to be having the same type of conversation, including the flight attendants. (I'd bet the pilots were in the cockpit kvetching too.) The details are always different, but the gist of the conversations is much the same—someone is bent out of shape by someone else's incompetence, arrogance, or obnoxious, mean-spirited behavior.

Restaurants, airports, family gatherings, parties, seminars, work-related get-togethers, grocery store lines, sporting events, elevators, bars, hotel lobbies— wherever you are, the background whine is there. I visited a friend in the hospital recently, and nearly everyone in the waiting room was griping about someone—the staff, the doctor, the sick family member, the other family members who weren't there, the DSL carrier, you name it. Virtually everyone, except perhaps the Dalai Lama, seems to be preoccupied with scrooges.

Although airing your grievances with others may help you feel less alone and on rare occasion gets you good advice, more often than not it keeps you stuck in a bad mood. While recounting every detail of the offending person's behavior, it's hard not to get riled up and feel the slight all over again. Our feelings are a reflection of where our attention lies, and if you are focusing on getting your listener to understand just how bad this other person has behaved, your energy is clearly on the misdeeds in question. It's hard to feel calm and happy when witty retorts have finally occurred to you and visions of revenge are dancing through your head.

What's more, time spent complaining is not time spent improving, letting go of, or preventing bad situations. It is sad to say, but griping does not accomplish a darn thing.

If venting to any and all who will listen doesn't do much good, what does? In the following pages, I'll show you some practical ways to deal with selfish, obnoxious, unethical, greedy, needy, mean people. I call them turkeys; you can call them whatever you like.

But as you read, my real hope is that you'll find it easy to eliminate much of your complaining. I can't wave a wand and ensure that you'll no longer have anything to complain about, but I can give you a few (make that fifty) better things to do.

Most of the strategies offered here are simple, but some might take practice to master. All of us have the bottom-line goal of keeping a smile on our face no matter what comes our way. This may sound like an impossible dream, but I've found that it really is possible.

I've developed these tools because life is challenging enough without giving the most irritating people in it power over our well-being. A huge part of feeling scrooged is feeling powerless. *How'd that happen? Why'd they do that?* But each of us has a vast reservoir of largely untapped power: we can change the way we look at, perceive, think about, and respond to virtually anyone. P.S.: scrooges *hate* this.

All the more reason to turn the page.

It's Not Daytona—
You're Not Jeff Gordon

Don't Try to Cook Tailgating Turkeys

Here they are—another set of holidays, another set of packed roads and parking lots, long drives to family gatherings in bad weather, and impromptu trips to the market when your cocktail party runs out of cocktail weenies. Holidays mean hitting the highways, and highways and roads can be unbearably jammed from Thanksgiving to whenever the last New Year's Day partier straggles home. There is a stocking-full of reasons the Most Wonderful Time of the Year can put us on the road—and in a rage. The holidays should probably come with a "DON'T DRIVE OR OPERATE HEAVY MACHINERY" warning label.

Anyone who's ever had an unfortunate encounter with an automobile knows they can do a lot of damage, especially when the people driving them just had a few drinks at their office party, or recently went to four toy stores looking for the only item their seven-year-old has asked Santa for, or have blocked their

1
*

rearview mirror's view with a big fat box. Sharing the road with these drivers (I know you'd never actually be one of them) can be scary and challenging in normal circumstances, let alone when you're feeling hurried and harried, overbooked and overwhelmed.

Our highest priority when strapped into metal and glass boxes traveling at high speeds is safety—not being right, not getting there first, and not teaching other people how to drive. So when someone's tailgating you, or you're navigating a four-way stop, or another driver near you is having trouble staying between the white lines, the safest thing to do is yield.

Too many people play games with tailgaters—slamming on the brakes, letting them pass, and then showing them how it feels by riding their bumper. But this is no game—it is life or death.

So yield, change lanes, pull over, and call the police, if you're really that heated. I mean this advice literally and figuratively. In case my symbolism isn't crystal clear, the preceding rules apply to the road of life as well as the road of ... well, you know, the road. Giving turkeys a wide berth is often the fastest and safest way to arrive safely at your destination. You may feel momentarily scrooged, but at least you won't have scars and stitches in this year's holiday photo.

So here are your keys. Enjoy the holidays.

Take a Vacation,
Not a Guilt-Trip

Don't Get "Should Upon"

They are *so* sneaky.

I'm talking about those insidious scrooges who present themselves as quiet, soft, concerned, and, on the surface, kind. They are the guilt-trippers, the people who, with a simple "Have you visited Joan?" or a quiet "I can't because I'm volunteering that day," make you feel guilty, persuade you to do what you don't want to do, and let you know that you should be doing something else, or something more. Ugh.

I just said that these people can "make you feel ...," even though I tend to avoid that phrase because I think it's important that we take responsibility for our own feelings and do as much as we can to avoid victim-think. But gosh darn it, guilt-trippers are so good at what they do that it's hard not to feel jerked around by them.

One reason they can so easily push our buttons is that often some tiny, deep-down part of us does wonder if we should be visiting Joan or volunteering

3

*

at the soup kitchen (especially if we're playing tennis or going to a matinee instead). We all know that self-doubts are a part of everyday life.

So let's say you are up against a fully conscious, stone-cold, semiprofessional manipulator. When I'm in this position, I sometimes think of a bumper sticker I once saw: "I WILL NOT SHOULD ON MYSELF TODAY." You might even try saying it out loud, with a smile on your face, to the person making you feel like crap.

Last year my family vacationed with two other families. I quickly realized that there was a guilt-tripper on this getaway. Everyone in his family seemed to easily agree on what they'd do when, except for Bill. I repeatedly overheard him pressuring his wife, sister, and kids to do the things he wanted to do by making it seem that they were things they should all want to do.

Now, this was Bill's vacation too, so he had every right to want to enjoy himself. But it was the *approach he used* to try to get his way. He didn't just say, "Gosh, I'm really interested in taking this tour. Any takers?" He whined, "I know you've all been there, but wouldn't it be great to be there together? This is a once-in-a-lifetime opportunity. Okay, I guess I'll just never see it."

Bill tried to make others feel sorry for him and guilty for depriving him. He did this to the point where they might not have been able to enjoy themselves unless they gave in.

Then I heard a beautiful thing. Bill's sister Judy said:

"Bill, you're acting obnoxious. We're all tired of being pushed around. We're going to do our own thing. You're welcome to join us if you can go with the flow and stop bugging us. If not, please just go and do your own thing. We all love you, but none of us want you around if you're going to continue to act like a three-year-old who isn't getting his way."

Consider the alternative: the family could have caved, had a lousy day, and resented old Bill. This way they didn't get their vacation scrooged, and Bill had the opportunity to meet his own needs and learn a little something about his behavior.

"Shoulds" happen, but you can send guilt-trippers packing.

Guest Room Grinches

Putting Houseguests from Hell on Best Behavior

During the holidays people travel from near and far to visit with the family and friends dearest to them. It's such a lovely portrait—everyone gathered at your house eating, drinking, and reminiscing ... while crammed together under one roof ... with the weather so bad you can't leave the house ... and you're sleeping (well, kind of) on the sofa so Mom can have the bed.... And by Day Two you're all sick of each other and the recycled, semi-sincere conversations.

Is it a Hallmark moment or the longest week of your life?

One thing that can tip the scales against a good experience is having guests who are, well, pigs. Whether they're visiting for an hour or a week, whether they're six months old or sixty years, blood relations or relative unknowns, if they leave wet towels on the bathroom floor and crumb trails, they can make you want to roll up the welcome mat and turn off the porch light.

Houseguests from hell don't make themselves at home, they make themselves on vacation—at a five-star hotel where they seem to assume that maid service occurs twice daily and all meals are included.

Alas, home invasions can take place year-round. Perhaps you play concierge during the summer months because you live near the beach. Whatever the season, it's time to reclaim your home sweet home.

The best way to do this is to make some rules and stick to them. Do this in the way that best suits your personality, but do it.

I know folks who have written up a playful list of do's (please help yourself to complimentary coffee and pastry whenever you get up!) and don'ts (please don't leave dishes in the sink!), framed it, and hung it on the back of their guest room door—just like at a Motel 6.

The point is that you can't expect people to read your mind. Stewing about how so-and-so really should know such-and-such without your having to mention it is fruitless. As Dr. Phil would say: how's that working for you?

So make it playful or serious, do it in print or in person, but one way or another, speak up.

When you're planning a get-together at your home, pipe up about what you want and need. If people are used to you doing all the cooking but you've had a really tough week (month, year), let them know that you are thinking potluck ("Could you please bring that wonderful stuffing you make?"). Or tell your guests that takeout is the plan this time around. Let them know that, because of your allergies, they just can't bring their dog this time. Since they probably can't kennel their hell-on-wheels three-year-old, make a plan to contain the chaos in one childproofed "wreck" room.

You might also try to silence your inner Martha and get over all notions of perfection. Paper plates diminish cleanup and increase the odds that your wedding china will survive until your next anniversary. And if you're debating whether to go with store-bought food or home-baked, remember this: if it gives you less time in the cooking room and more time in the living room, it's a good thing.

As you may have gathered by now—and may not like—I'm suggesting that you can't just mutter resentfully under your breath (which makes *you* the scrooge); you have to take responsibility for your needs by sharing them. Your incentive, aside from feeling less like a put-upon maid, cook, and babysitter, is time and space to experience the true spirit of the season, the genuine good feelings you have for your guests, and pride in your home—which, apparently, is *the* place to be.

Now put those houseguests from hell on their best, rather than beastliest, behavior.

✳ Dodge the Oddballs

Some People You Just Have to Avoid

Have the holidays ever driven you to near insanity? How about that time you kept crossing paths with that well-known scrooge in your family or circle of friends? Did it almost push you over the edge? As the saying goes, doing the same thing over and over again and expecting a different outcome is the definition of insanity. If we repeatedly put ourselves in the path of scrooges we *could* avoid, we are certifiably nuts. If the offending person is so (fill in the blank), why on earth do we keep putting ourselves in his or her line of fire?

I know, I know, it's not that simple. However, there are plenty of times when avoidance would do the trick, when we could choose to go around or otherwise dodge these nincompoops, whether we find them in our workplace, family, or neighborhood. Yet more often than not we don't, thinking that such a choice on our part gives them some kind of power. Why should *we* change our habits or at all inconvenience ourselves?

To stay sane and happy, that's why.

Those in addiction recovery learn to avoid the places—bars, drug-buying neighborhoods, gambling casinos—where they suspect they might slip up. Why not take people who bum you out this seriously?

Let's say there's a café where you love to while away the occasional hour with the newspaper or a good book. You've gotten to know the folks behind the counter, you love the way they make your double cap, and it's conveniently located. The trouble is that you aren't the only regular. Another patron, who seems to be there every time you are, repeatedly approaches you and clearly wants to be your new best friend. He won't take a hint when you don't really respond to his questions. And when you've said you are at the café to enjoy some alone time, he's accused you of being standoffish.

Do you keep going to this café, crossing your fingers that the coffee monster won't be there? Do you grit your teeth and blandly respond every time to his litany of queries? Do you assert yourself and ask him to buzz off—and then endure his dirty looks? Or do you simply find a new café?

I think you know what my answer is. What do you have to lose, especially since it's become hard to even enjoy the place?

When I described this avoidance technique at a speaking engagement, a woman named Barbara approached me and tried to defend her decision to keep picking up prescriptions at a pharmacy where the woman who had an affair with her husband shopped. And it wasn't just that they both shopped there: somehow it happened that they routinely shopped at the same time and regularly needed refills on the same day. "Why should I change my routine for that ——?!" the woman asked me. "You wouldn't be changing your routine for her," I replied. "You'd be changing your routine for *you*." She instantly got this, marveling at how she'd been torturing herself for months for no good reason.

So stop the madness. Dodge the oddball, avoid the creeps you can, and you might just find yourself going sane.

*

Do as Columbo Does

*Playing It Cool
over the Hot Apple Cider*

O ne of the things that make scrooges so frustrating is that we can't quite figure them out. *Why* are they being mean or greedy or self-centered? *How* did they get to be obnoxious, angry, or arrogant? *What* is their behavior all about?

Entertaining such questions for any length of time will land you a date with the Excedrin bottle. After all, if the answers were obvious, these folks wouldn't be so difficult. So instead of giving yourself a migraine, I'd suggest that you chuckle, shake your head—and think of Columbo.

Yes, that Columbo. I enjoyed this classic television detective show mainly because of the delightful behavior of the rumpled, trench coat–wearing sleuth (played by actor Peter Falk) when collecting clues on a case. Invariably, he'd be talking to someone who'd say something that didn't add up. But rather than getting upset, he'd acknowledge his puzzlement, scratch his head, and chomp on his cigar.

We can emulate Columbo (minus the cigar perhaps) when someone is acting strange or in some distasteful way. Rather than getting irked, we can be benignly befuddled. Rather than getting frustrated, we can choose to be calm and curious—like a detective on a case. You might still wonder what the turkey's behavior is all about, but with your metaphorical trench coat on, you're a Columbo scratching your head, not a victim pulling your hair out.

A few days ago I was pulling into a parking space on a crowded shopping street near my house when a woman darted across a double yellow line to try to poach the spot out from under me. Maybe she hadn't seen me at first—though how you can fail to see a car pulling into the space you're heading toward is beyond me—but when she did finally see me, she jumped out of her car and started screaming. I don't think parking places are worth raised voices, so I told her she was welcome to this one. But my response seemed to make her even angrier.

I was certainly puzzled. I suspected she was upset because she felt entitled to the space, but the magnitude of her emotions was a mystery to me.

I avoided getting as angry as the person screaming at me by focusing on how curious her behavior was. *How strange,* I thought. *How interesting even.*

But—and I think this is key—I felt no need, unlike Columbo, to *solve* the case or crack the mystery of her emotions.

I don't play a detective on TV, and neither, I'd bet, do you. Let that nut case go unsolved. He or she is not in your jurisdiction anyway.

Have Dessert,
but Skip the Poison

Forgive or Die

Some people are constantly rehearsing. Not for a part in a play or a job interview. I mean rehearsing the wrong some scrooge did to them. It's natural to spend *some* time questioning the actions and motives of someone who hurt you. Ideally, these thoughts are fairly fleeting. Yet all too often, as I well know, we don't reflect on the incident for a few moments and move on. Instead, we spend hours, days even, cooking up our own holiday "stew."

But while you're think-think-thinking yourself into an ever-fouler mood, tossing every sideways word and minor offense into a growing soup of resentment, consider this: *you, not the offending person, are the one who is suffering.* I can practically guarantee you that the other person gave no more than a passing thought to having offended you and probably didn't even notice. While you're having endless "take that!" conversations with this person in your head, in which you always have the brilliant last word, you are really only talking to yourself.

So why not think for yourself instead? Recognize that while other people and their actions will affect your thoughts and feelings, ultimately those thoughts and feelings are your own. And while you might want to scream, "But it's his fault!" like a grade-schooler on a playground, you can't expect other people to fix what runs through your own head and heart. That's your job.

The way to get this job done is really very simple. Pause. Step off the hamster wheel and observe your thoughts. Realize that these thoughts have just caused you to do twenty minutes of cardio but haven't affected the situation or the other person one little bit. Is this really how you want to spend *your* time?

This is essentially what I did when I was doing business with a large company a number of years ago. They received their fees from the services I provided, and I was to get a royalty for those services. The problem was that this company had—I learned too late—a long history of unethical practices. My reputation was being seriously damaged through this affiliation.

I had a legitimate gripe with these people. The trouble was that my fight with them was hurting me.

I was bitter and angry and could feel the stress in my body. I wanted to feel free, not at the mercy of so-and-so for doing such-and-such, so I ultimately chose, not to let the jerks off the hook, but to let myself down from the hook my anger had me on. I quit rehearsing their wrongs. I quit rehearsing my rights. And I freed myself by thinking for myself.

You can too. Dump the stew. Enjoy yourself.

Handling Cruella
the Salesclerk

With Customer-y Kindness,
Everyone Wins

T hey are the gatekeepers who stand between us
and the things we want. They are clerks, salespeople, customer service reps, the folks on the other
side of the counter or the other end of the phone. They
have more power than most of us would like. The
power to make our lives easy or hard, our errands
pleasant or tedious, and getting through our to-do
lists a breeze or a bad scene. Around the holidays,
when we have more to do and they have more of us to
deal with, it's easy for them to feel like the customer
is always wrong. So the kindly gatekeeper transforms
into Cruella Deville.

A friend of mine was moving his family into a new
house and setting up the basic services. All was going
fairly well until it came to the phone. He was attempt-
ing to set up three lines, one for him and his wife, one
for the kids, and one for the Internet and fax machine.
While speaking to the customer service representative,

he ran into a roadblock. The woman told him it was going to be three weeks before he could get his service going. She read him something out of the "rule book" and refused to budge or bend one bit. Worst of all, she seemed to enjoy the power she had to disappoint and inconvenience him.

When my friend said that he couldn't possibly wait that long, the rep became angry. "Look, Mr. Smith, that's the best we can do—take it or leave it." My friend tried again, this time using a more personal touch. He said, "I'm sorry, and I know you have a tough job. It's just that I have three small kids, and it would be dangerous to not have phone service for three full weeks. Is there anything I can do to speed it up? Most of my friends have service within a day or two."

For whatever reason, this explanation made the clerk even more irate and defensive. She dug in her heels and said they would be out there to install the phones as soon as they could. Long story short, three *and a half* weeks later, the phone service was turned on.

What could my friend have done differently? The best remedy I have found is to speak to the supervisor of a clerk in scrooge mode. The last time I did this, here is what I said: "Thank you, Mrs. Jones, for taking my call. I have a serious problem, and I'm so grateful you're here to help me solve it. You see, I'm having a surprise party for one of my children, and the plan is to have all the kids watch a movie at home at the end of the night, but our television isn't working. I was told by your employee, who I know is doing her best, that there was no way to get the problem fixed in time. I'm hoping, since we still have four days to go, that you can find a way to make it happen. I'll rearrange my schedule around yours and will be a grateful customer if you'll work with me on this."

What I was doing, other than being honest and polite, was giving the supervisor a reputation to live up to. My specific words aren't as important as the way they created some rapport with the supervisor so that she would be on "my" side." In this instance, it worked like a charm—a cable guy was out the very next morning and had the problem fixed in thirty minutes.

Sometimes you're not so lucky. But remember: most supervisors have supervisors of their own. As long as you can keep your cool, the rest is about rapport and patience. Rapport is a very powerful tool, not as a form of manipulation but as a way of connecting with another person. Once that connection is made, the person you're working with will do everything in his or her power to help you. It's just the opposite of what happens when someone gets mad at you for having an edge in your voice or for expressing any frustration whatsoever. If clerks suspect that you don't respect them, forget about it. And really, considering the number of turkeys that clerks encounter in a week, shouldn't we respect them from the get-go?

Practice a little customer cheer and you'll increase your chances of being satisfied—rather than scrooged—every time.

Be a Hum-Bug

Sing Your Way to Happiness

One of my all-time favorite grocery checkout clerks works at a store near my house. I was in there one day when a customer came to her line and began throwing her groceries on the conveyer belt. This customer had "bah humbug" written all over her face as she grinched and grumbled.

I was so impressed with what I saw my clerk friend do. Rather than engage the customer in any way, my friend simply started to sing in a friendly, tasteful tone. I didn't recognize the song, but it was peaceful, happy, and comforting.

At first, the grump looked at the clerk as if *she* were crazy. This scrooge was so uptight that even this benign gesture seemed to bug her. But after a few minutes the customer began to visibly relax. She became much friendlier and seemed to let down her guard. If I'm not mistaken, I even saw her smile.

There's a big difference between a humbug, and a *hum*-bug. I've noticed that people who let a little melody into their lives can change grinches into good guys.

When we remain calm and happy in the presence of those who are definitely not, our positive energy rubs off on them. It's a fact of life, just like static electricity. Singing ushers in that atmosphere of calm and happiness. It's sort of like playing the banjo: it's hard to be depressed while you're doing it. Think of the way Maria's singing calms the kids during a rainstorm in *The Sound of Music*—or the way the Whos down in Who-ville ultimately touch the Grinch's heart with their singing.

The next time you're face to face with grumpy people, try something similar. Instead of joining them in their land of woe, subtly invite them into a sunnier climate. Present yourself as a person who is content and likes life. Smiling to yourself and humming a tune are two ways to do this. (Babies seem able to comfort and amuse themselves this way for hours.)

I asked my clerk friend if she often sang in the presence of a difficult person, and she said that she did. She said it really helped keep her immune from the effects of their negativity. Even if you aren't in the best of moods yourself, acting as if you are—whether by smiling or singing or simply making a conscious effort to unfurrow your brow—can help you get there.

I tried something similar the other day. I was talking to a very aggressive man who seemed to be very angry at the world. I began to smile and hum one of my favorite songs. Much to my surprise, my humming had the almost identical result often obtained by my clerk friend. The angry man became noticeably calmer and much more pleasant. I don't think he had the slightest idea why he was having a change of heart, but I'm certain that my own good feeling was rubbing off on him somehow. If a bad mood can rub off on others, why not a good one?

Give a little whistle or hum a tune this holiday season. At worst, people will think you're crazy and leave you alone. At best, you'll brighten somebody's day.

25

*

✳ Take Back the Wheel

Don't Let Scrooges Hijack Your Mind

Each one of us has a mental steering wheel, but
sometimes we hand it over to a scrooge. "Just
thinking about a scrooge, or of a recent encounter
you've had with one, is enough to make you feel nuts.
You could be walking your dog or sitting in a meeting, and suddenly you find your thoughts going off
in a totally unwanted direction. The scrooge has just
wrested control of your mind.

The secret, then, is to become more aware of your
thoughts so that you can take back your "drive" time.
Surprise yourself sometime and tune in to the many
thoughts filling your mind at any given moment. In a
way, it's wonderful that we can be having dinner with
a friend and simultaneously add an item to our grocery list or plan what we'll do when we get home. But
it's not so great to realize that thoughts that bring us
down pop up as regularly as spam on e-mail or tele-
marketers on the phone. The good news is that, unlike
with spam and phone solicitors, simply becoming

aware of annoying thoughts goes a long way toward eliminating them.

Suppose, for example, that there's someone at work who seems to live to undermine you. He's your least favorite person at work. But you're at home now. The workday is done, you're cozied up on your couch, and the only thing you have to do is have a pleasant evening with your family.

Then the key turns and the engine starts—you've started thinking about that jerk at work. Images of the latest sneaky maneuver by the coworker from hell roll by like scenery. Your brow is knit, your blood pressure is rising, and you haven't heard what your spouse just said. All this while you're safe at home and the coworker is nowhere in sight.

What I call "frustration recognition" is simply the process of realizing when this kind of thing is happening. Once you tune in and realize that *it's your own thoughts,* not the coworker, wreaking havoc with your evening, you are back in the driver's seat. You can't control what other people do (especially people who aren't even there!), but you can control your thoughts. Especially with practice, you can bring yourself back into the present—perfectly comfortable—moment.

It's disconcerting and even humbling to recognize how easily our own minds can be carjacked. But it's also a testament to the tremendous horsepower under the hood. If we can accelerate toward the brick wall of a bad mood, we can also stamp on the brakes. So take the wheel, downshift back into the moment, and let yourself enjoy the real-time scenery around you.

Agree and Be Free

Turning a Jerk into a Pal

Some turkeys just love to fight. They seem bred for confrontation. They can't have a conversation without voicing a controversial opinion or making a critical comment. They may say they just believe in blunt honesty or in standing their ground, but actually, for a variety of reasons buried beneath their feathers in their pink turkey hearts, they see everyone as an opponent. They say and do outrageous and provocative things because they've learned that when they do, nine times out of ten they get their "opponent" mad enough to start sparring. Once they get this desired response, they're happy—or at least they're back in their confrontation comfort zone.

Imagine, however, that this turkey has a tennis racket (use your imagination) and is hitting a tennis ball against a backboard—back and forth, back and forth. Then, all of a sudden, the backboard disappears. What can he do? He can't continue hitting balls; he has to find another game.

When you learn to "agree and be free," you are the disappearing backboard. If you disagree with a bully or try to defend yourself, the confrontation will continue. You can't win, however, because the jerk just wants to keep the game going. Since people like this are such a pain, the nonsense they're dishing out certainly doesn't deserve to be dignified by any reply. So agree and walk away. The game is over—and guess what? You win.

You might agree by literally saying, "Yeah, you might be right," or by not disagreeing, or by simply smiling and nodding. The trick is to get over the feeling that, by not pounding the ball back, you're letting this kind of boor win. You need to realize that by *stopping* the game, you've won it. This is really the only way to triumph against those who'll do anything to keep things stirred up.

Here's an example of what I mean. I was at a deli not too long ago, waiting to order a sandwich. When it was my turn, the man behind the counter called, "Number thirty-one," and I raised my hand. At that instant, one of these "pick a fight" types jumped in front of me and claimed he was next. The counter man, knowing this guy hadn't been in line, took an angry tone with the interloper. Bingo! The bully had gotten a rise out of someone and was now off and running, belligerently standing his ground. But I threw a wrench in his plans by calmly telling the man behind the counter, "It's okay. It's his turn." Some would say that this was weak of me, or that I taught the bully he could get away with bullying, or even that I'd done wrong by lying.

Fine. What I know is that I prevented a two-way—and possibly three-way—fistfight. The creep who jumped in front of me seemed capable of worse things, and hey, the sandwich maker was holding a knife. I got my lunch a lot quicker than I would have if I'd let the altercation escalate, and lunch, after all, was what I went to the deli for.

Leave aggressive turkeys for the barnyard. Agree, be free, and go about *your* day.

Hades or Homecoming?

Opt In — or Out — of Family Events

Iknow people who have complained for twenty-five years about their family gatherings. They gripe because for all those years they've gone along with a tradition or ritual—whether a Sunday dinner or an annual Thanksgiving trek across the country—that makes them miserable.

For the most part it is not a question of love—the majority of us love our families even if they drive us batty on occasion. Some relatives, however, are people we simply "put up with." And then there are those we'd like to prune right off the family tree!

John loved most of his family dearly, but the bad apples he wanted to shake off the tree were two cousins he described as "coming from a different planet." At family gatherings, this pair always managed to stir the pot, get drunk, become aggressive, and say inappropriate things. You get the idea. When they were around, John's mood plummeted, his stress level soared, and he wanted to get out of Dodge as soon as possible. This scenario occurred over and over again for years.

Finally, reality whacked John on the head. He realized that he could pick and choose, that he could attend only those gatherings that didn't include the infamous turkey twins.

John began to ask about the guest list whenever he was invited to a family event. Would the cousins be there? he'd ask tactfully. If the answer was yes, John would make a polite excuse and decline. If the answer was no, he'd make an effort to attend.

He tried his best to be flexible, making an exception for important events when his absence would hurt or offend. Most importantly, he maintained his peace of mind when he encountered his bad cousins at weddings, funerals, and baptisms. Because John was making a *choice* to attend, he no longer felt at the mercy of his cousins' behavior.

During the holiday season, however, we might feel that we can't pick and choose our family gatherings. This feeling that we can't control how we spend our time and who we spend it with can make us dread the holidays. We can become filled with "bah humbug" feelings and miss out on enjoying the family and friends we do treasure simply because of a few bad apples. Our apprehension, however, simply isn't necessary.

The situation isn't black-and-white, and we don't have to stop caring about our own sense of well-being from Thanksgiving through New Year's. The happy compromise is to enjoy and create gatherings during which we can take care of ourselves *and* show our loved ones we care. Go ahead and prune away the situations and people you've learned are unpleasant; savor the family traditions you love; go out on a limb and create new traditions that include the people and practices that make you happiest. By recognizing your right, even within your family, to pick and choose, you can be both grounded in your roots *and* free to branch out and grow. Try it.

Tune 'Em Out

When Not to Listen

The first time I suggested this method to someone who was tired of dealing with a loud and talkative person, I was accused of being a Pollyanna.

But hear me out. There are really two ways to listen. The first is the way we usually think about listening: concentrating on what's actually being said. We focus so that if someone were to quiz us, we could repeat the gist of what we've heard. We listen this way when the content of what's being said is important to us—such as when we're taking directions at work or in school, or when we are learning something new.

The other type of listening is more passive. It's the type of listening we do when we're enjoying music, when we're relaxing, and when we know there *won't* be a quiz.

It's extremely helpful to use this more passive style of listening in the presence of a loud, "look at me" type. You still hear the person, but you aren't actively taking in the words. You aren't focusing on the content of the speaker's nonsense, and so it can recede a bit, like background music.

I call this "cruise control" listening, because you aren't sitting there stewing over some boor's nonsense. You are present, but not fully engaged, and not taking it personally.

Here's an example. Recently I was on an airplane flight, and the person sitting next to me was drunk—as a skunk. He reeked of alcohol, and he wanted to talk. In fact, he would not be quiet. What made the encounter particularly awkward was that he recognized me and claimed he liked my books. At any rate, had I paid close attention to him or thought at all about what he was saying, it would have been a miserable flight. But I minimized the misery—in fact, I almost eliminated it all together—by simply changing the way I listened to him. I didn't ignore him, so I wasn't disrespectful in the slightest. Instead, I simply listened with my heart and not my head.

There was no need for me to pay attention to the content of what he was saying, since it was drunken gibberish. Indeed, focusing on the content would only have upset me. Yet there was no need for me to be rude. That would have surely upset him—and we all know that no good can come of upsetting a drunken man on an airplane. No, I simply listened very softly to whatever it was he was saying, the time passed away—and I ended up not feeling scrooged.

Cruise control listening is a powerful way to distance yourself from a difficult person. It is somewhat like ignoring someone, but takes far less work on your end. Ignoring is an active and extreme response, whereas this technique is ideal for dealing with people who are needy, obnoxious, loud, or demanding more attention than you are prepared to give. Like turning down the volume on a radio, or switching from AM to FM, *you* work the control—and keep your cool.

*

Picture the Perfect Encounter

Could You Actually
Enjoy *the Scrooge?*

Many of us are highly skilled at anticipating the worst that could happen. We imagine embarrassing ourselves at a party or bungling a presentation at work, and the thoughts can be so vivid that our stomachs churn and we cower in our cubicles, a slave to our nerves. As a result we never try new things.

But if our powers of imagination can do all this, can't they do positive things in the reverse? Can't we create visions of competence and success that we find calming and encouraging?

My anticipation of a big, important meeting where several of my not-so-favorite people would be in attendance had me frowning every time I thought about it for weeks.

Finally, when I caught myself wasting another ten minutes fretting as visuals of conflict and dissent danced through my head, I decided to give equal time to painting a more positive mental picture.

In addition to my usual preparation for the meeting, I spent a few minutes visualizing the event going off without a hitch and everyone getting along wonderfully.

I closed my eyes and imagined myself at the meeting, start to finish. If a bad scene popped up, I consciously put a positive spin on it, looking for a way it could work out well. I imagined the meeting going smoothly and anticipated how good I would feel after this success. I concentrated on picturing the people I was worried about acting like perfect gentlemen.

I'm no magician, but as it turns out, my visualization pretty much came true. The meeting went well, and the people there behaved beautifully.

As I say, I don't believe I possess magical powers, but I have come to accept the mysterious power of our minds. I have found not only that we can bring on bad outcomes by doing nothing but dreading and imagining them, but also that we can encourage positive outcomes by doing the opposite.

You don't have to understand how visualization works (I don't fully) to have it work for you. Athletes do it all the time. Spending some concentrated time really seeing and feeling yourself pitch a strike, serve an ace, or sink a putt can subconsciously train your mind and body to do just that. Adding visualization to your usual prep work for just about anything—from sports and public speaking to sleeping and lowering your blood pressure—sets the scene and plants the seeds for success.

A bonus benefit that is nothing to sneeze at is that while anticipating the worst can make us physically tense and anxious, visualizing success tends to leave us relaxed and optimistic—feelings that can pave the way for our optimal performance.

There are lots of good books and tapes out there on the subject of visualization, but you can 'give the basics a try anytime. When you anticipate feeling scrooged by an impending encounter, take a few deep, slow breaths. Picture the person or event in question and imagine the best possible scenario. Try to see it all in great detail—sights, sounds, smells. Feel yourself being relaxed and confident, smiling and happy, in that future scene.

Feel better now? I bet you do. Your future can be "pictured" perfect if you turn that worry around and drive it backwards.

Go to Your Room!

When to Call A Time-Out

Suddenly double-crossed by a coworker in a meeting, sideswiped by a driver while running errands, stung by a friend or family member's unexpectedly harsh words—we usually get scrooged in an instant, out of left field, with no warning. In fact, speed and surprise are part of the power of the scrooge.

But stop before you respond immediately. There's a time and place for dealing with what that turkey dragged into your life, but my best advice is the same as what some parents tell their kids: go to your room and take a time-out. If you don't, you may worsen an already bad situation.

Feeling wronged sets off our adrenaline and our instinctual fight-or-flight mechanism, but pausing puts us back in control, creating a sense of spaciousness, choice, and calm. It often makes the difference between reacting like a hothead and responding like the cool, enlightened type you aspire to be.

Taking an appropriate and well-timed pause gives you perspective *and* the upper hand because, instead of resolving matters by "evening the score," tit-for-tat responses tend to up the ante and keep the action-reaction ball in increasingly hostile play.

A pause is a very easy thing to do. Pretend you're a scientist and observe your initial, instinctual desire to "punch" back. Then pause. Perform the proverbial count to ten, maybe in the high school Spanish you barely remember. Breathe. Then observe again and you'll probably find that your heat-of-the-moment, largely physical reaction has cooled a bit. Now your heart and head stand a chance of getting a word in edgewise, and you can choose to act in ways that won't make you cringe later.

Suppose, for example, that you learn that your child is the only kid in class not to be invited to a birthday party. My guess is that you'll instantly be furious and hurt. If you go with those feelings and react, the problem can quickly escalate. Who knows what you might do? Get on the phone with the other parent and begin a confrontation? Seek out some type of revenge?

But if you pause between the moment when someone does something you don't like and the moment when you respond, you may very well see things quite differently. You may realize that an innocent mistake has been made, or that there is some very good explanation for what has taken place. With the birthday party, for instance, there may have been no ill intentions whatsoever. And here's the really important thing to remember: when you are calm, even if there was an actual intention to exclude your child, you'll be in a far better place emotionally to deal with it. Perhaps you'll decide to call the birthday child's parent and see whether you can work something out so that your child can go to the party, or you may decide to drop the matter, figuring that the best way to help your child through this difficult experience is to use it as a teaching tool.

One thing is absolutely certain: you'll better deal with a scrooge's slights, in ways that don't turn *you* into a scrooge, if you take a time-out first.

Don't Dance

Avoiding Arguments,
Tangos, and Worse

Turkeys make awful dance partners. When you're confronted with a mean, obnoxious, or otherwise difficult person, think about it: that person *needs* you to fulfill his or her mission, which is to bother you. They want you to play Ginger Rogers to their Fred Astaire. If you refuse to be bothered, that goal goes unaccomplished. It really does take two to tango, and nothing frustrates irritating people more than someone who has the wherewithal to sit out their dance.

There's an adage that applies here: would you rather be happy or right? This question is easy for me to answer. I have no problem allowing a wannabe scrooge to feel "right" if it keeps me from getting miserable. I've learned over the years that I'd much rather stay happy than spend even a little bit of time trying to prove I'm right or argue with a turkey with ruffled feathers.

Here's a real-life example of what I mean. I was doing some early Christmas shopping for my daughters when one of the most disrespectful and obnoxious customers I've ever encountered entered the store. She approached the young salesclerk and began to complain and issue commands. It was quite an unpleasant sight to see.

But the clerk was wiser than her years. She maintained her poise and simply said, "No problem, ma'am. I can help you find exactly what you're looking for." Rather than take offense or give the customer a dose of her own rude medicine, the clerk attended to her business. She skillfully had the woman out of her store—and out of her hair—in minutes. She seemed to know that there was nothing she could do to change the cranky customer, and also that she had a choice as to whether or not she would "buy into" the crankiness. If the customer was looking for a fight—and she surely seemed to be—she was out of luck.

You could argue that the clerk had a right to feel wronged and that she would have been justified for responding in kind. Yet the clerk did not fall for that faulty logic. She took the high road, the road all too often less traveled—and that really did make all the difference.

As I watched the encounter unfold, I couldn't help but think that the clerk is probably a pretty happy person in all aspects of her life. She certainly seemed to know that it's important to pick your battles—and that most battles aren't really worth fighting at all.

When you put being happy above winning or being right, you get to feel happy, now. When a turkey tries to trot you out onto the dance floor, take a pass.

Call a Lawyer

Last Resorts

W hat are five hundred lawyers at the bottom of the ocean? A good start.

We've all heard the jokes, but haven't we all some- times wished for someone to stand up for us, fight for our rights, or just serve as a buffer between us and the scrooge du jour?

My sister and a number of my friends are lawyers, and they have a good sense of humor about their profession's reputation—which is somewhere between used-car salesman and politician. But when we're dealing with an impossibly difficult person—someone dishonest, dangerously angry, or simply too irrational to communicate with—we might very well need legal counsel to get to the other side of the dispute.

Whether confrontation has already begun or you just sense it's inevitable, a good lawyer (or profession- al mediator) can be your middle man (or woman) who takes you out of the line of fire, gives you clearheaded advice, and helps you to keep your cool.

I recently met a man named George who had plans to sell his triplex. The only problem was that one of his tenants refused to move out. The tenant's lease had expired, and it was legally time for him to leave, but he would not budge. George tried everything— talking with the man, reasoning with him, and even giving him several extra months to find a new place to live. To show his goodwill and good faith, George even offered to help the man find a comparable new rental nearby. Still the tenant refused to vacate, stubbornly stating, "I pay my rent, and I'm not leaving." George's patience ran out when he realized that no matter what he did, this man was unwilling to negotiate, reason, and move on.

Finally George called an attorney who specialized in this type of dispute. He learned that there was a specific legal process to follow and that, while he could do it himself, the attorney could guide him, deal with any new problems that cropped up, and generally free him to get on with his own plans. The attorney would shoulder the burden.

Turning to an attorney is a last, not a first, resort. Our first choice is not to spend money on legal fees or be adversarial; we'd prefer to work things out on our own. But realizing this is not always possible is key to feeling less scrooged by the irrational, the vindictive, or the just plain scary. Realizing this saves us from beating our head against the proverbial wall, getting

angrier—and more bruised—with every move. And remember: hiring an attorney is not like declaring war
or challenging someone to a duel. Yes, some scrooges
seem to thrive on and create confrontation, but your
legal advocate can *prevent* this by defusing a volatile
situation.

Best of all, working with a lawyer can help you
achieve goals that are every bit as important as solving the issue—such as maintaining your composure
and even your compassion in the midst of conflict.
Legal advice may be necessary, but hostility is not.
Lifted out of the maddening stalemate with his tenant, George may (at least eventually) feel compassion
for the inconvenience and personal upheaval his tenant is experiencing in the midst of an unwanted move.
So *before* push comes to shove, keep your cool and
consider calling your lawyer. It's a valid path of last
resort that can keep you from getting scrooged.

Love the Players,
If Not the Play

*Accepting the Obnoxious
in Spite of Their Act*

There's a difference between what a turkey *is*, and what a turkey *does*. One of the very best ways to keep yourself from being bothered by turkey-ish behavior is to learn to discriminate between a person and his or her actions. In fact, this may be one of the only ways to keep from becoming a humanity-hating scrooge yourself.

At a spiritual level, all of us are one and the same in God's eyes. But we don't live solely on a spiritual plane. We're spiritual beings having a *human* experience here on earth. Because we're human, each of us has a unique personality and experience and history. We all have our own strengths, weaknesses, fears, hopes, and dreams. We all do some things well and need help in others. And while we are each unique, there is one thing we have in common: we all make mistakes.

We may be perfect in God's eyes, where it counts, but all of us have human imperfections. The more we reflect on this notion, the easier it becomes to let go of the things that bother us about other people. The trick is to realize that it's possible to like or love a person and still be annoyed by or even furious with his or her behavior. The action and the actor are not one and the same, and we do not need to treat them as such. As we learn to differentiate between the two, the edge is taken off of our irritation. What's more, we gain the opportunity to see that the other person is just like us—imperfect.

Let me show you what I mean. I was walking my dog Ty when two women approached me with their two large, unleashed dogs. As we came fairly close to one another, one of the women yelled out, "Don't worry, they're friendly." Not two seconds later, both of their dogs started racing toward me and Ty. They growled and bared their teeth, and though they didn't actually bite us, they came very close. They were anything *but* friendly, and I was suddenly pushed up against a hedge. One of the women called out cheerfully, "No, no, Clyde and Toby, come here, boys." That was it. No apology, nothing!

Quite frankly, I was too shocked, and it all happened too fast, to do anything about it. The women and the dogs were around the corner before I knew it.

Then, as I regained my composure, I began to stew about what had happened and about what could have happened. And boy, did I get mad. My mind was spinning in circles as I reviewed what I should have said and what the women should have done.

Luckily, within a few minutes a little bit of wisdom came to me. I remembered the importance of differentiating between the action and the actors. Yes, I thought it was irresponsible of the women to be oblivious to their dogs' behavior. I was angry at their action—or more accurately in this situation, their inaction.

But I reminded myself that these women were two beings just like me who were blind about a certain aspect of their life. I told myself that although I would never allow my dog (if he were mean) to be off of a leash, I have done plenty of other things that have irritated other people. But that doesn't mean I'm a horrible person—it just means I have faults and blind spots. I would hope that most people who know me believe that to be true. And my guess is that most people who know those two women feel the same way about them.

This reminder enabled me to separate the actions from the actors. I didn't have to stay mad at them—or at myself—for not saying or doing something differently. I learned to appreciate the players, even if they were improvising badly on the stage of life. Because we're all in this show together, and nobody gets all their lines right.

And besides, I had better things to do that day— like walk my dog.

Let Go, Let God

Exchange Lower Impulses for a Higher Power

When you're confronted with a difficult person, you might feel the weight of the world on your shoulders. *"Why me?"* you wonder. *"Why do I have to deal with this?"* Well, you don't—at least not all by yourself. You can give that turkey away. Many people sum up this bit of mental magic with the mantra "let go, let God." You needn't believe in any particular God to try this trick. "Letting God" can simply mean relying on the wisdom of the universe.

The words "let go, let God" are extremely comforting when put into action. Some people visualize handing a bundle of their burdens over to someone else; some have a literal "God box" in which they file troublesome issues. The idea is to let go of the notion that you need to figure out "Why me?," that you really should have all the answers, and that you are all alone in your struggles.

Claire had one of the most irritating neighbors I've ever heard of. He watched the road like a hawk and felt that the road belonged to *him*, not the other half-dozen neighbors. He even called the police when neighbors received deliveries because he disapproved of the weight of the trucks coming up the road. And he also routinely sent letters threatening to sue Claire and her family for ridiculous reasons.

Claire, a wise and spiritual person with a good sense of humor, chose not to fight with or become overly frustrated by this man. She did this by turning the situation over to God, who she figured had more coping skills. She also reasoned that since God had the big picture, the fact that she had this neighbor meant that she needed to learn something from him or from the situation. (Don't worry if you can't muster this level of spiritual perspective all at once.)

Sure enough, Claire's hunch was spot on. In the past (before she got all-wise), Claire had been a bit like her neighbor—aggressive, prone to take offense, ready for a fight. By living so close to this kind of "mirror" of her former self, she saw firsthand how distasteful her behavior had been. She vowed never to backslide into her old ways.

What's more, because Claire herself had at times behaved somewhat like her neighbor did, she felt not only less bothered by him but also a little

*

compassionate. She wished him well because she knew that being at odds with the world and in a constant state of agitation was not fun. She wished him peace—and felt peaceful within herself. Sound too good to be true? Let go and you just might leave room for God's blessing.

Remember to Breathe

Unruffle with Quick Meditations

Having meditated for more than twenty years, I find that it's not only one of the most important parts of my life but perhaps my best defense against difficult people—especially when I'm preparing to see one.

Meditation keeps me centered and calm, nonreactive, and in a place of inner harmony. Quite simply, when I finish meditation, it's downright hard to be irritated by anyone—no matter how difficult they are. And that's not because I'm pretending to be above it all or gritting my teeth or aiming for some kind of lofty, super-evolved state of being. No, no, and no. Being unruffled is simply the result of meditation for me. Perhaps it can be for you as well.

I can't presume to teach you how to meditate in the space of a short chapter in this book (though the practice can be a lot less complicated than you might think). But I do hope to pique your interest, give you a taste of its benefits, and perhaps send you in the direction of a book, tape, or class on meditation.

When you learn to meditate, the same things and people that would normally drive you nuts will have almost no impact on you. There are exceptions, of course, but because meditation has so many other benefits as well (greater focus, lowered blood pressure, and perhaps even some protection against the memory loss that so often accompanies aging), you have nothing to lose and much to gain by trying it.

Many think that to meditate you have to adopt some weird religion or philosophy, or that it requires a huge investment of sitting-around time. Although there are many forms of mediation, this simply isn't the case. (There's even a walking meditation practice for when you just can't sit still.) Pretty much across the board, meditation is simply learning to still your mind, to be present in the moment (rather than obsessing about the past or worrying about the future), and, as the Beatles sang, to "let it be." The goal isn't to become passive or oblivious but to truly harness your powers of awareness and to waste less time living in the past or the future.

Meditation can be done in as little as eight minutes a day. (See Victor Davich's eight-minute meditation at www.8minutes.org.) The amount of time you devote to it isn't as important as trying it and finding a routine that works for you.

The payoff of meditating with some regularity is almost like exercising a muscle. Over time you become better at controlling your thoughts and reactions and less at the mercy of them. It's a gentle but extremely powerful kind of strength.

You can see how this toned and strengthened muscle might come in handy in dealing with the difficult. When I need to meet up with someone who has pushed my buttons in the past, I routinely prepare by meditating for ten minutes. Unlike dreading what could go wrong in the meeting or replaying what has gone wrong when we've tangled in the past, meditating helps me arrive at the meeting feeling calm, composed, and certain that I can handle whatever the moment brings.

So try meditation and you might find yourself on vacation from aggravation.

Expect Less, Enjoy More

When You Give Up Hope, You'll Feel a Lot Better

A wise friend recently pointed out how strange it is that people get rattled by situations whose outcome they already *know* will be less than ideal. "I can understand being irked by unexpected problems, but not by known variables," he said. The example he used was traffic. Everybody and their mother dislikes gridlock, but if you know that your morning commute or a certain intersection is always slow, why not just make the necessary adjustments? Leave your house earlier, buy books on tape to listen to, or find a carpool or a different route. The expected delays may still be there, but they'll be *expected*—and you'll be prepared to do something other than just groan.

If you know you'll be put on hold for twenty minutes when calling your health insurance carrier, or that visits to the DMV or your doctor require long waits, *and* you take some action to make these delays less annoying (doing a household chore while you're on hold, or bringing a great book to the waiting room), you're bound to feel less scrooged. You knew it was coming, and hey, you were right.

What so many of us do instead is indulge in a kind of magical thinking. *It always takes thirty minutes to get to work, but it should only take fifteen minutes, so maybe today ... My doctor always makes me wait, but perhaps this time it will be different.* I'm not suggesting that we expect the worst but that we be realistic, using past experience as a guide and planning accordingly.

Many of the difficult people in our lives are known variables, as predictably grating as the traffic slowing down every day at 7:45 A.M. at that certain bend in the freeway on our way to work. Why be surprised when the irritating irritates?

Here's an example of how this works. Last year at tax time, Jeff told me he needed to call the IRS to get information and straighten out a problem on his return. He smiled when he told me he was sure that the call would take a while, that he'd get transferred to several different departments, and that he was always on edge while making such calls because, after all, hard-earned cash was at stake.

Jeff made his call, but this time he was prepared. He used a portable phone and headset and accomplished many other tasks throughout the call. His call was indeed transferred several times, and the whole transaction took the better part of an afternoon. But he was still smiling because, while he might have wished it could all be wrapped up in an easy five minutes, he wasn't surprised by the time that was actually involved. It was pretty much what he'd expected, and he was ready. In fact, Jeff was far less stressed throughout the day because of all he was accomplishing.

We like to be prepared, to know what's coming our way. This gives us a feeling of security. Lousy surprises await us all, but think about it: many of the people and situations we let under our skin have given us full warning. Instead of feeling scrooged, become savvy. Learn from past experiences—don't expect to go the speed limit during the morning commute, and don't look for the surly clerk at your favorite bookstore to suddenly become Suzy Sunshine—and plan accordingly. Expect less, enjoy more.

Get Mad,
but Not *That* Mad

*Temper Your Temper
for the Holidays*

Years ago I was having lunch with a brilliant mentor of mine who had become a great friend. I was ranting and raving like some cable news host, basically arguing for my right to be really, really ticked off about a variety of things. It was as though I were pleading my case before a court of law and wanted the judge, my mentor, to conclude that I was absolutely right to feel exactly as I did. I wanted a person I respected to validate my mood.

But the judge did not rule in my favor. My friend was his usual calm self when he said, in a very loving but firm manner, "Richard, I understand why you are mad, but why *so* mad?"

"Why *so* mad?" Such a simple phrase, but it flipped the switch in my mind. Others have told me that those three words gave them "lightbulb moments" as well.

There are so many ways for people to let us down. And just as my friend didn't tell me that I shouldn't be angry or disappointed, I won't tell you that. But do we have to get as mad as we do?

We may think we don't have any control over the degree of hurt or anger we feel. Feelings just happen. But that's the beauty of "why *so* mad?" It stops the runaway train of our feelings for a moment, and often, by simply stopping to notice and question them, we *can* change—or at least diminish—them.

The goal is perspective. Is your anger proportionate to the slight? Is there some reason that *you* are reacting the way you are, never mind what *they* have done or said? If 'you're having a bad day, or grappling with an illness in the family, or struggling at work or with your finances, something that might not normally get under your skin can become the excuse to let off unrelated steam. Are you angry because of what someone has done, or because it's the fifth time that person has done it? Asking "why *so* mad?" not only helps you understand what you're feeling but nine times out of ten takes quite a bit of the oomph out of those feelings.

I had the chance to observe this when I was on hold with my phone company for an hour and fifteen minutes. After about fifteen minutes, I was impatient. After forty-five, I was pacing the floor, my mind filled with all sorts of angry thoughts—I was going to change carriers and read the rep (if one ever picked up!) the riot act. I was going to write letters and speak to supervisors because somehow, some way, I had to get someone to compensate for my valuable lost time.

While I was pacing, my eyes fell on my favorite photo of my daughters. It sounds corny, but this reminded me that the world was not out to get me; I had a pretty darn good life. I stopped pacing. Even though I was still on hold, the runaway train of emotions was stopped. Rather than just feeling furious, I could *observe* that I was furious, recognize that I was in the middle of an annoying situation, and ask myself whether I really needed to be as wound up as I was. I ruled against it. My darn good life didn't need to be derailed by the phone company.

There are certain questions in life—"why *so* mad?" being one of them—that seem to answer themselves. The wisdom is built into the question. Sure, it was irritating to be on hold for the length of a feature film, but let's face it, there's no reason I should be exempt from such irritations. No one was out to get me personally, and though it certainly was too long to be listening to Muzak versions of classic rock, this kind of thing happens. I decided I didn't have to be

"so mad" about this and wrote replies to a few e-mails
while I waited for the phone company rep to find me.
I felt better, the problem was eventually solved and I
tempered my temper, which made everybody feel better—starting with me.

Be Mad About What You're Mad About

Don't Unpack Last Year's Griefs

We usually think we know exactly what we're feeling scrooged about. A friend is late for your date and you start to fume. The cause and effect seem perfectly obvious: when friends are inconsiderate and rude, you get annoyed. 'Nuff said.

Sometimes, no doubt, you are mad about precisely what you think you're mad about. As Sigmund Freud presumably said: "Sometimes a cigar is just a cigar." It is what it appears to be, pure and simple.

But this catchphrase caught on because Freud was a master at unmasking deep, subconscious meanings and motivations. The phrase works because lots of times a cigar isn't just a cigar, or is really more than a cigar. Sometimes when we think we're mad about A, we are really, largely, mad about B.

Here's what I mean. Your friend is late, and you're annoyed. You managed to get there on time, so why can't she? But let's say that when you were in elementary school your mother was supposed to pick you up at school at 3:00 every day but rarely got there before 3:45. This made you feel really lousy. You were embarrassed by it (did she forget she had a kid?), a little bit scared (as all your other classmates cleared out and you were left alone), and sad (were you really not important to her?). Mostly you were mad at her for evoking all these unpleasant feelings. Why couldn't she get her act together?

Now, twenty or thirty years later, you are probably better able to understand how hard it was for your mom to be on time, but that doesn't do anything for the sad, mad, scared kid down deep. And now, all these years later, while waiting for your friend, you actually don't mind having a few moments on your own with your coffee. And you know your friend is coming from across town and probably facing traffic congestion. But still, you find yourself steamed.

So what if some portion of the steam coming out of your ears is really ancient history steam from all those lonely afternoons after school when you were a kid? You might say you just hate waiting and find late people rude, but perhaps a good part of the reason why you hate this kind of behavior is your own past experience.

All kinds of things can trigger us this way. Raised voices can unconsciously remind us of squabbling parents, people who clam up can evoke the way old family secrets were kept, a negative review at work can recall a poor report card at school, and on and on.

One of the best things about being willing to make these connections is the two-for-one bargain you get: with your adult perspective, you get to heal old wounds, and with your insight into the past, you get to feel less wounded in the present.

If your current anger feels just a tad bigger or deeper than the current offense deserves, take that as a clue and do a little detective work to see what's underlying it. When you get mad, it pays to stick to the subject so you don't transform into the scrooge.

Let 'Em Steam

Other People's Anger Isn't Always Your Problem

Most of us want to be kind, considerate, competent, and responsible. But perhaps we want even more to be *thought of* as kind, considerate, competent, and responsible. The idea of anyone anywhere being mad at, disappointed in, or hurt by us can make us so uncomfortable that we routinely put our own needs and wants last. We wind up feeling scrooged by our fear of being someone else's scrooge!

But nobody—not ever—can please 100 percent of the people 100 percent of the time, and when you try, you wind up in a straitjacket that you were never supposed to wear. You may come to resent people, jobs, or other situations you otherwise enjoy. For instance, maybe you have a friend you love dearly but who always seems to have a pressing personal problem that she needs to work through on the phone with you just when you are facing a big deadline with a work project. If you aren't willing to let her down on occasion, I can guarantee that you will end up feeling resentful at the way her needs always trump yours.

A while back I made a number of commitments on the same set of days. I wanted to do all the things I agreed to and to please the people asking. But when those days grew near, I realized I couldn't possibly do it all. I got on the phone and tried to get out of or postpone as many of the engagements and appointments as possible. Most people were quite gracious.

But several others were simply furious with me—and let me know about it in great detail. I felt bad about overbooking myself and then letting people down, but I had to accept the consequences. Even though I made the appropriate apologies, I now had to accept that not everyone was going to forgive me.

I hung up the phone, sat at my desk, and tried to think this feeling through. I realized that I needed to accept that some people were not willing to forgive me. And while that was disappointing, I then thought about how I routinely meet dozens of obligations, keep my word, and live up to expectations. I'd bet that I—and you—can be counted on about 90 percent of the time. That's not a bad average.

Focusing on the one time in ten that you can't follow through is unfair. You don't need to do it to yourself, and others shouldn't do it to you. When you make a mistake or otherwise can't follow through—when you are, in other words, human—you should apologize and then forgive yourself, even if someone else isn't willing to do the same. After you have apologized and made any other amends reasonable in the circumstance, other people's decision to stay mad at you falls into the really big category of things you can't do a darn thing about. Their anger becomes their issue if they decide to cling to it, not your fault or your responsibility.

I'm not suggesting that you get into the habit of letting others down. (Although when you're feeling scrooged by your schedule and the number of people who "need" you, it is a good idea to reexamine your commitments and priorities.) But one way to avoid feeling scrooged by others is to be less fearful of being perceived as a scrooge yourself. Say no when you need to, apologize when you should, and then let yourself off the hook—even if the other person, for whatever reason, won't.

The Benefits of
Selective Intolerance

Taking Your Family to Obedience School

Take a moment and think about the people in you life who rarely get scrooged. Are they just lucky, or have they done something to achieve this state of grace? I think it's something else. I think these people have taken their friends and colleagues to obedience school and taught them not to jump all over them or run them around. This technique won't spare us from the many bad wild cards life can deal, but there is one huge area of human behavior that we can control—we can teach others how to treat us.

Without sounding too flip, it's like training a pet. People who rarely get scrooged seem to be the ones who make it clear to others, through their words and actions, what they will and will not tolerate—just as good teachers do when they greet a new class, or as smart parents do raising their kids. These people say and show, "I will put up with this but not with that." They set fair, clear, consistent boundaries, stick to them, and don't feel bad or guilty about doing so. When someone disregards their instructions, they gently point out the error and reiterate that they will not tolerate such things. They might do this with words, or an e-mail, or by walking away, or, after repeated episodes, by ending the relationship. They set limits and stand by them.

Many species of scrooges can be thwarted this way. Some scrooges have a sixth sense for pushovers, whether in routine encounters with friends, family members, and employers or in more sporadic contacts with neighbors, clerks, and other businesspeople. They hone right in on someone who will tolerate their rudeness, unreliability, selfishness, or even abuse. If they have to choose between someone who has boundaries and someone who doesn't, you can guess where they'll head. But even if you have developed a bad pattern with someone you have known for years and are likely to know for many more, you can change the rules—and teach new lessons.

I have two friends who dealt with the same real estate agent in the last year. The first, Jerry, thought the agent was aggressive, pushy, opinionated, and "the most difficult person he had ever worked with." Jerry had his reasons for working with this agent, but he always felt walked over and pushed around after their encounters.

The second friend was Anne. She had the same opinion of the agent but also had reasons for wanting to work with her. The difference was that Anne had the wisdom and courage to teach the agent what she would and wouldn't put up with. She sat down with the agent and had a frank chat about the way she wanted and needed things to work.

As you can guess, Jerry felt scrooged every time he met with the agent, but not Anne. Anne had learned how to practice selective intolerance. She took that agent to obedience school.

Even when you think you are dealing with an "impossible" person, it pays to look at your own behavior. Have you bothered to make your displeasure known? Have you set a limit and stood by it? Or have you just silently stewed and complained to other people?

Not everyone is "teachable," but if we don't even try, we have only ourselves to blame. The good news is that we have the power *and* the responsibility for teaching others how to treat us. We are not helpless, tossed about on the rough seas of life. We are not victims. It is often the case that we have somehow "taught" the offender that it's acceptable to treat us badly.

Case in point: years ago I had a friend whom I very much enjoyed. But there was one thing he did that drove me nuts: he virtually never stopped talking. I think it's great when people can tolerate moments of silence, but such moments seemed to drive my friend to fill-fill-fill them up. With nonsense if need be. It was driving me crazy.

Then it occurred to me that I had never told my friend that his nonstop chatter bugged me, that I liked natural silences and lulls, and that I thought these were even a testament to closeness. I did not want to hurt his feeling by telling him, essentially, to shut up once in a while, but if I didn't I knew I would soon stop wanting to be around him.

It wasn't comfortable to have this chat, but I did it. I told him how much I valued our friendship and admired him as a person. I then prefaced my comments by saying that I had something important to share and that I hoped he would take it in the spirit in which it was intended: to make our friendship even better. I told him that I loved communicating with him, but that as a quiet person I needed some silence between our words.

Waddayaknow—it worked! We're still friends, and now we share wonderful moments of silence between enjoyable stretches of conversation.

To the extent that you can (which might be greater than you think), train the folks who "dog" you how to behave. Yank the leash gently when their behavior goes out of bounds. There's nothing rude about it. It's just part of keeping everyone involved—yourself included—from getting scrooged.

Keeping Your Identity
— And Your Wallet

*Safeguarding Your Finances
from Identity Thieves*

About the only good thing you could say about
Ebenezer Scrooge, before his eventual epiphany,
was that he mostly left people alone. He was miserly
and selfish, but he didn't mug people.

But a certain type of modern-day scrooge does mug
people: they are identity thieves. These invasive scoff-
laws aren't content to mutter, "Bah humbug," as they
pass you on the street—they want inside your wallet.
And with increasing and alarming frequency, they do
just that, faster than a Santa on SlimFast can slide
down a chimney.

Identity theft is coming soon to a neighborhood
near you, and if you haven't been a victim yet, watch
out. It has been called the "fastest-growing crime in
America." According to a study by the Gartner Group,
one in fifty consumers has suffered identity theft. And
I can tell you firsthand that identity theft is something you want to avoid. I bring it up here because,

as with so many other forms of scrooging, it really is something you can go a long way toward preventing.

I'll give you a few important, commonsense tips on what you can do to protect yourself, your finances, and your credit history. But part of my goal is to encourage you to pursue this subject further. Talk to your financial advisers, do a Google search, and read articles or the appropriate chapter in a financial well-being book. Don't view this as tiresome research but as savvy self-care. You can keep extreme scrooges from tangling your finances and life into a worse mess than last year's Christmas lights.

I had to pick up the pieces after I experienced an identity theft. My hope is that you won't have to do the same if you are proactive about protecting yourself. Here are some basic tips I learned from the police, a private detective, and a number of books and articles I've read:

* Check your credit report once or twice a year. You are now entitled to a free copy of this report. Contact one of the three major credit bureaus—Equifax, Experian, or TransUnion. Check for errors and report them immediately. What you're looking for are transactions like someone opening up credit card accounts in your name or, worse yet, getting

home or car loans. Checking your report regularly is also just good financial health maintenance. You may not know your credit score, and you may have never seen your report, but others (insurers, banks, landlords) read up on you all the time. Make sure that what they are reading is accurate.

* While you're making friends with the credit report people, chat with them about getting "red flag" service on your account. Qualifying rules vary, but this makes it nearly impossible for an identity thief to open new accounts in your name.

* Make a list—and check it twice—of all the credit cards you have, the account numbers, and the phone numbers you need to cancel them. Put all this info in one safe and secure place. Have pass codes put on all of your cards so that only you will have access. Make your code something other than what an identity thief might guess at (birthday, street name, etc.).

* Take your social security card out of your wallet. You don't have to memorize the number and then eat the card (though you have committed the number to memory by now, haven't you?), but you need to realize that this number could be an un-

scrupulous person's passport to your money. Share the number as rarely as possible. Ask whoever is requesting it if the last four numbers will suffice. The fewer people who have your number the better.

* This may be tough—and you may want the frequent-flier miles—but use your credit cards sparingly. It only takes one bad apple—or the bad apple's girlfriend, coworker, or boss—to make the meal or sneakers you paid for by credit card extremely expensive. Most people are honest, but some are just sloppy. Where does your card go when someone walks off with it to process your purchase? If you do use your cards a lot, it is especially important to check that credit report.

* If your wallet or purse goes missing, don't forget to notify the DMV about your lost license.

* Think about how secure your mail is. If it magically falls into a safe place in your home every day, great, but if it gets left in a communal or unlocked mailbox, get a lock or a post office box. I once returned from a weeklong vacation to no mail, even though I had not asked the post office to hold it. I had no idea what had been there—credit card bills

perhaps, or new credit card or home loan offers. This is coveted data for a thief; many identity thefts originate with your mail.

These suggestions are just the tip of the iceberg, meant to get you thinking—and acting—about ways to foil criminal scrooges. Precaution, not paranoia, is the plan; keeping your money and your sanity is the goal. The last thing you need around December 25 or any other time of year is someone traipsing through the mall pretending they're you. Be generous with your own friends and family, but don't let others be "generous" for you.

Quit Being Your Mother *

Ban Worry from Your Holidays

Irecently received a greeting card with a sentiment that resonated with me. It says, "Worrying does not empty tomorrow of its troubles, it empties today of its strength." I thought about how we spend more time worrying about obnoxious people than we do seeing them, talking to them, or actually dealing with them. They take up more space in our minds than in our days. So I want us do some mental spring cleaning.

When we worry about scrooges, two very important, very negative things happen. First, we lose our sense of well-being. When we're caught up in our thoughts about how obnoxious someone is, we waste our mental energy thinking about things that may not even happen. It was Benjamin Franklin who once said: "I worried about many things in my life—a few of which actually occurred."

Every year or so the cranky neighbor of my friend Sarah made vague but menacing threats about the easement they shared. Stay tuned, he seemed to be saying, because one of these days he was going to sue. The legal action never materialized, but still my friend worried about the potential hassle, expense, and possible outcome.

What did Sarah's thoughts accomplish? Zero. Zilch. Nada.

This brings us to the second point about worrying. Suppose you're worrying about seeing an ex-boyfriend or ex-girlfriend tomorrow. Let's even assume that it really is going to happen and that it's not going to be pleasant. It's a drag, but you are going to have to deal with it—*tomorrow*. In other chapters, I talk about some constructive ways you might anticipate such a meeting, such as visualizing an ideal encounter, but hear me on this: worrying is simply not constructive.

Worrying today about something you have to deal with tomorrow just makes today a drag. You *may* have this interaction in person tomorrow, but you don't have to have it today in your mind. Really. Isn't having the dreaded encounter once, in real time, enough?

I'm not trying to be casual about it, and I know worry is a hard habit to break—but it's worth the effort.

The same logic holds true *after* you've dealt with a difficult person. Think about it. Let's say you've now had that confrontational meeting with your ex. If you continue to worry about how it went, about what you said and didn't say, about what your ex said, about the possible repercussions, you're essentially having the unpleasant encounter again, over and over again. How productive is that?

I'm all for *dealing* with difficult people in all the ways we are talking about in this book. But I'm not for worrying about them. "Worrying does not empty tomorrow of its troubles, it empties today of its strength." So quit acting like your mama, or your grandma, or your constantly vexed aunt. Instead, go on a cleaning spree and clear the worries from your mind. You'll be making room for much nicer things—like the pleasure of the moment—when you do.

Give the Gift
of a Second Chance

Let Others Prove They've Changed

When you've built up personal history with a scrooge, it can color every present interaction. No matter what this person says or does, you are reading the past into every action and syllable. Even if this person is being perfectly cordial, you think, "Aha! He or she is laying a fresh trap for me, setting the stage, trying to bring my guard down so that I can be scrooged anew—maybe even worse than before."

Pretty soon you've built up a conspiracy theory worthy of Lyndon Larouche.

But it takes energy to steel yourself for fresh offenses that may never come. It's hard to go through the holidays playing the part of interpreter, turning your suspect's conversation into scrooge-speak in your mind. It's unpleasant to feel like you must watch your back—the whole time. You end up deflecting the good as well as the bad. Yes, it's wise to learn from the past, but it also makes sense to live in the moment, to quit being so twitchy, to approach even a proven scrooge with open eyes, ears, and heart.

That means, among other things, not reading from yesterday's script. Assume that the last time this person scrooged you, he or she was going through something difficult that had nothing to do with you, but you were there and got caught in the crossfire. There have certainly been times when someone else has found you acting kind of scroogey. We all do it.

In a fresh encounter, this previously difficult person has a chance to show you his or her better side, like the loving Scrooge who came out of hiding after being visited by the ghosts of Christmas past, present, and future.

Giving someone a second chance and the benefit of the doubt does not make you a sap. Your openness and receptivity might even bring out the best in someone who is just a diamond in the rough.

I formed a very negative impression of a fellow named Jeremy in a neighborhood association I recently joined. He seemed self-righteous, and I thought the ideas he voiced were, well, dumb. After a few months of going to these meetings, I had occasion to have a one-on-one conversation with Jeremy, and I found him delightful. In that encounter, he had really bright ideas about an issue I was having and didn't seem smug at all. He told me how passionate he was about the problems that had brought the group together, and why. I decided I'd misread him: I'd read between the lines and made far too many assumptions. I almost felt I owed him an apology.

Give your scrooge a shot at an Extreme Make-Over. You may (or may not) always be pleasantly surprised with the person's actions in the future. But giving a second chance is what you would want someone to do for you. It would make a great gift this season.

The Punk Band
Next Door

How to Handle Noisy Neighbors

Quiet, sneaky, passive-aggressive turkeys are bad—but aren't loud, disruptive birds even worse? Some people suffer with neighbors who have noisy pets or screaming children, play ear-splitting music, throw wild parties, yell at each other regularly, or even just keep their television volume at dance-club level. What's to be done with inconsiderate people who make noise when you are trying to sleep, work, or relax?

Don't go passive on this one. By now you should know I don't recommend fuming silently about the selfish people next door. Don't leave anonymous notes, snip their cable TV wires, or poison their dog. Instead, speak up about their need to pipe down.

As we learned in the last chapter, I recommend giving people the benefit of the doubt. It's hard to believe sometimes, but some people just live on a volume of "10." They don't have a "5" or a "2" on their personal volume knob. Maybe they grew up with lots of siblings, or deaf parents, or next to an industrial factory. Maybe loud gives them comfort. Maybe, by now, they are hard of hearing themselves.

Or maybe they just hate you and want to ruin your life with constant, grating noise. I think this is probably not the reason.

The first thing to do if you live or work next door to noisemakers is to enlighten them: "Hey, that's really loud and it's interfering with my thoughts/phone calls/sleep/religious reflection. Can you take it down a few notches?" If this works, be really noble and follow up with a note or small gift of thanks; rewarding good behavior helps ensure it will continue.

On the other hand, if you don't get any satisfaction, do what your congressperson does and build some coalitions. Are other neighbors or employees as annoyed as you are? Gang up. Write a group note or e-mail. Exercise your power in numbers.

And try being specific. The inconsiderate are often clueless that their actions are bugging anyone. You might need to spell out what you'd like: "Please tell your dogs that 3 A.M. is not the best time to practice their howling," or, "It would be nice if you and your wife didn't start the house party when most people are entering REM sleep."

My editor's assistant, Lisa, once lived in an apartment building where she had a terribly nice—and noisy—neighbor. Sounds and sleep disruption that you can't control and that you believe are caused by inconsiderateness can make you climb the walls. Lisa was scaling hers on a regular basis—when she wasn't pounding on them out of frustration.

For purposes of alliteration, let's call the noisy neighbor Nate—nice Nate. Nate had a work schedule that had him up all night. The TV would go on around 11:00. He also liked to regularly reach out and touch some relatives—he had in another time zone—a time zone that made calling them at 3:00 A.M. optimal. Moreover, Nate seemed to think that when speaking to people over the phone long-distance, one must yell to be heard. Nate's feeding schedule was also interesting. Meals involving large numbers of pots and pans had to be prepared around 1:00 A.M. The pans seemed to get washed—with water running, plates and pans banging, and Nate singing over the running water—around 4:00 A.M. Lisa got a good sense of this routine because she was awake through most of it.

Why call him "nice Nate" with all this going on? Because whenever Lisa knocked on his door to ask for some peace and quiet, he couldn't have been nicer.

Would you like some of the curry I'm cooking? he'd ask, or, do you want to come to a party tomorrow night? Nice questions, but apparently he was deaf to her reasonable requests.

So Lisa finally went for her last resort: she told on him. You might have to do the same. When other options fail, don't be afraid to call for backup. There's nothing shameful or childish about protecting your sleep schedule and peace of mind. Apartment managers, work supervisors, and even the police may not be your first call, but they might have to be your last. You may feel guilty about ratting out your own nice Nate, but a good night's sleep should make you feel a whole lot better about it.

Retail Therapy

When Rude Customers Share the Grief

Service isn't what it used to be, and maybe it never was. But customers aren't what they used to be, either. When two people meet for a meaningful transaction at the cash register, the scrooging can go both ways, especially during the holidays.

Annoyance with clerks and waiters is, of course, built into the shopping equation. While some clerks and waiters are perfect angels, others are perfect devils, and they seem to come out en force from November 23 through January 5. There is the salesclerk who treats us as an intrusion as she stares off into space or makes personal phone calls. The cashier who makes a cash register mistake and doesn't bother to apologize. The waiters who pour us regular instead of decaf or give us the onions we asked them to hold, and the clerks who only bother to bag half our purchases.

But having seen life from the other side of the counter, I'm here to tell you that the customer is *not* always right. And given the fact that no one, except perhaps mail carriers, works harder than store clerks during the holidays and has so many customers (read:

crybabies) to deal with during this time, it makes sense to put yourself in their shoes (along with their aching feet) for a few moments.

I admit I'm biased in this regard. Many of my friends, family members, and acquaintances have worked in retail over the years, and as I write this my sixteen-year-old daughter is in her first summer job. She loves the job so much that she hopes to keep it during the school year. But she has had her share of customer scrooges, even in the summer months.

A particular crummy customer comes to mind. As my daughter tried to help her, this customer complained about everything—the merchandise in the store, the prices, the music playing over the sound system, how long it took anyone to greet her when she walked in. She had a smiling, anxious-to-help clerk listening to her, but she didn't seem to really want to feel any better or have her needs addressed. She wanted to complain. To make matters worse, she knocked over and spilled a bottle of lotion. She may not have done it on purpose, but she did purposefully laugh at the mess she'd made and storm out of the store.

This is an admittedly extreme example of a really troubled and troubling shopper. But clerks encounter more routine annoyances hourly.

Clerks, salespeople, and waitstaff of all kinds need a strategy for dealing with the run-of-the-mill rude and the off-the-scale obnoxious. The strategy I'm offering here takes less than a minute and can be done anytime, anywhere. It's something you can do when you have to share airspace with, or even serve, an offensive person. It's a way to shield yourself from that scrooge's bad vibes.

My dear friend Sheila Krystal, a brilliant psychologist, taught me this technique. You simply imagine two circles of light in a figure eight. You're in one circle, and the scrooge is in the other. Imagine a pen or pencil tracing the outer lines of this figure eight, slowly, around and around. See yourself safely within the lines of your circle and see you-know-who staying put in the other one, bound by the lines you are repeatedly reinforcing.

I love this strategy a lot, for several reasons. It gives you something to do when you can't do much else. It gives you a time-out, calming and centering you. It really drives home the boundaries idea. And it's peaceful and gentle—you aren't picturing your tormentor burning in the fires of hell (are you?), but instead in a circle of light *away* from you.

You may sometimes have to share space with a toxic turkey, but you can always put him or her in a boundary bubble. So much more mature than closing your eyes, sticking your fingers in your ears, and chanting, "I can't see you, I can't hear you," don't you think?

Let Jerks Be Jerks

Forgive and Forget

Your assignment for this holiday season and beyond: forgive that bum. You know who I'm talking about. He or she has had enough power over you and your heart. Get some relief. Unpack that bag full of anger, hurt, or resentment you've been lugging around. People are tired of seeing you with it—*you're* tired of seeing you with it. There's no payoff in unforgiveness. It's a loser's game. Your feelings will never change the other person, and they can't undo what he or she did to you.

Tough medicine—and medicine I have had to take. I was conned in a business relationship once (well, at least once). It hurt me very badly because I had put a great deal of trust in the other person involved. It took me a while (I had to go through a slew of other feelings first) but ultimately I was able to genuinely forgive the duplicitous guy. As soon as I did he had no more power over my well-being. Yes, the jerk was a jerk. And yes, it really had happened. But I was now free of feeling bad, mad, and sad. The memory of the deceit is not my *favorite* memory, but it no longer rankles like a popcorn kernel lodged between two teeth.

My relief had nothing to do with the other person, or with what he did or said. I never even told the lout that I had forgiven him. The whole process took place solely within me.

Let me make something completely clear: I would never do business with or otherwise trust this person again, no matter how frozen over hell became. In fact, I doubt that I'll ever speak to him again. But that's about the extent of my residual feelings, which otherwise are almost nonexistent, or at least neutral—neither positive nor negative.

Choosing to forgive someone who has scrooged you doesn't preclude taking other appropriate action—speaking your mind, severing ties, even initiating legal action. But I do think you have to forgive that person at some point for your own peace of mind. Otherwise that backpack full of bitter feelings will turn you into the sour-faced scrooge. Let jerks be jerks, and let them go their way.

Professional Victims and Need Monsters

When to Rescue, When to Walk Away

At a dinner party I attended recently, at least half the people there were dealing with terribly difficult situations. One had a teenager in rehab, the husband of another had recently been arrested, and the mother of yet another had just attempted suicide. Oh yes, and there was also a woman who had been dealing for a year with a chronic, debilitating illness that had cost her a job.

Sounds like one heckuva party, doesn't it?

Those of us present who were not in crisis felt, as you might imagine, a tad overwhelmed. So much pain and so much need around one dinner table. I believe everyone there had the same goal: to support and feel supported and to enjoy what can be enjoyed (good times with good friends) even during difficult times. I think everyone there got what they wanted and needed from the evening. Those who had sad stories to share and needed compassion, advice, and even practical help, got it. Those in supporting roles were able to feel a bit useful.

But as I travel around the world speaking to groups and listening to audiences, I often hear variations on a complaint: so-and-so needs so much, she's like a vampire, I always feel mad and guilty after listening to her barrage of woes.

All of us find ourselves feeling extremely needy at various times, but there are those bloodsuckers who seem to have made being needy their vocation. They are professional victims, and the rest of us are supposed to be their full-time rescuers.

This type isn't an easy scrooge to handle because the situation the eternal victim presents us with is gray rather than black-and-white. Needing and receiving are integral to relationship. Relationships are deepened and strengthened by our ability to express need and accept help, and vice versa. The problems arise when one person in the relationship seems to think the only way to get any attention is to be in crisis. Or, on the flip side, when one person feels useful and productive only when saving someone's butt. You often find these two types married, and hey, if it works for them, great!

But the situation I hear about most often from people is the one that arises when they are just going about their business, trying to be a good human being, and they get ambushed by a friend, relative, or acquaintance who continually needs someone to lean on.

Sometimes rescuing a person is the least loving thing you can do. Lending an addict money, for instance, might just keep that person drunk or loaded. If we repeatedly drop everything and run to the rescue, we might be reinforcing an unhealthy pattern. If we always save Vince the Victim, what incentive—or opportunity—does he have to learn to save himself?

Healthy needing and healthy giving is another thing entirely. The folks around the table I described needed a lot from each other and gave a great deal to each other—time, the loan of money, transportation, legal and medical expertise. But I don't think anyone felt helpless or imposed upon.

If you are feeling scrooged by someone's neediness, take a few quiet moments to think about the situation. Is this person always calling 911? Like the boy who cried wolf, that can surely make it hard for us to take the crisis du jour seriously. Is all your time together or on the phone spent talking about the needy one's horrible situations? If you never get a word in edgewise about your own life, this isn't much of a relationship. Do you often feel manipulated into doing things you don't want to do, can't really afford to do, or don't reasonably have time to do? How friendly is that on the part of your "friend"?

Then scrutinize your own behavior. Have you participated in this lopsided need-and-rescue pattern for a long while? Do you (admit it) like being needed? Would you have anything to talk with this person about if not for the all-consuming problems?

If the answers to these questions have given you a much clearer picture of the dynamic between the two of you, the solutions are probably obvious. You have to learn that not every emergency has your name on it. Not every fire alarm is your call to duty. You might need to change your own behavior or ask for changes on the other person's part. You might have to learn to say no—and then stand your ground, not feeling guilty when you have nothing to feel guilty about. You might have to accept being branded as "mean" instead of thoughtful and generous. And you might ultimately have to walk away from this person altogether. Sometimes that's what we *and* the other person need most to grow and be well. That's a true rescue.

Turn Hissing Cats into Purring Kitties

Strategies Against Defensive People

Though difficult people come in many varieties, they all seem to share one characteristic: defensiveness. Their threat level is constantly on "red." They go through life with a figurative gas mask on and their riot shield up, afraid of what (or who) might strike them next. Their sense of extreme vulnerability and weakness—puts them on guard even against people who love them.

Their defensive attitude makes them offensive.

Don't worry—I'm not trying to defend the defensive, just to understand them a bit so that we can work around them.

Defensive people have a sixth sense about when you might be working up your nerve to offer them a gentle criticism or suggest a perspective other than their own. Before you can say, "Boo," they'll tell you, "No, I'm not," "You don't understand," or "How dare you?" Case closed before it's even opened. Their behavior and motives simply cannot be questioned. Ever. Unfortunately, they do not extend the same courtesy to you. Your every move is suspect to them because you might be getting ready to say or do something that would jeopardize their precarious perch; they'll do anything to protect their little patch of ground, including making regular preemptive strikes.

The defensive are tough to deal with, no doubt about it. If their arms aren't literally folded across their chests, with their chins jutting out and their feet firmly planted, they might as well be. This posture makes it natural for us to get defensive in return, becoming stubborn, lashing out, dispensing tit for tat.

Sam, a good friend of mine, had a relatively minor car accident in which, luckily, no one was hurt. It was Sam's fault, and he was very apologetic to the person he hit. He assured the other driver that he would take full responsibility for getting his car fixed. But Sam could barely make himself heard over the furious ranting of the driver. He assumed that Sam would not take responsibility and that he might even try to shift the blame, so he came out of his car swinging. Maybe this driver had had a similar experience in the past, but in his determination not to let it happen again, he was unable to see (or hear) that this time around the other party was very cooperative.

Sam handled this man's defensiveness beautifully. Rather than getting angry at his accusations and becoming defensive and aggressive in return, Sam let the driver rant and rave until he got it out of his system. Sam knew that trying to make himself heard would only result in both of them yelling louder. When the driver calmed down, Sam reiterated his sense of responsibility and his plans to make everything right. Seeing that he wasn't in mortal danger, the driver could finally let down his guard. He actually wound up reassuring Sam that "these things happen."

Another important strategy with people always on the defense is to use "I" statements instead of "you" statements. "You sure are drinking a lot of eggnog these days" is likely to send the defensive into sullen denial or angry retort mode. "I have a hard time having just one cup of this stuff" might open the door to a friendly little chat about just the thing you want to talk about: self-medicating, addiction, cholesterol, eggnog recipes, whatever.

Making "I" statements is actually, come to think of it, not a bad idea in most situations. "You make me sick" is rarely a productive conversation opener, but "I feel queasy when you ..." might be. "I" statements show you taking responsibility for your own perceptions and feelings, not making assumptions or accusations.

But wait a second—what if you do want to be critical of someone, even if you know that person is extremely insecure and defensive? Sugarcoating your conversation, however, isn't dishonest; it's practical. (Haven't you found that hiding your cat's antibiotic in some good tuna works better than grabbing her, prying open her jaws, and stuffing the tablet down her throat? Mine always spits the pill into my eye when I do that.) Approaching the defensive with more delicacy than you might approach another person is just plain smart.

Speaking of cats, you might borrow the same technique with defensive people as you use to coax a kitty over. Remain calm, move slowly, refuse to give back what you get, and reassure the scared bully that you aren't a threat. I've tried this with defensive people on several occasions, and though I've walked away from the experience thinking the other person didn't hear me, or that the conversation went poorly, the next day I received an appreciative call or note. Defensive people really are just scared most of the time. Treat them as such, and you might turn a hissing cat into a purring kitty.

Taking On
Teams of Turkeys
Dividing and Conquering
Troublemakers

The only thing worse than one incompetent, arrogant, or mean-spirited turkey is a whole gang of incompetent, arrogant, or mean-spirited turkeys. If you've ever been attacked by turkeys (and hasn't everyone?), you know it can feel like a rumble straight out of *West Side Story*—without the tunes. Unfortunately, such rumbles have become a public menace and can occur anywhere—at home, at work, in school, even in your neighborhood. In spite of local pet laws, wild turkey gangs still roam freely.

I've ripped one effective strategy, not from the headlines but from TV detective shows. Adopting the role of an interrogating officer, you can play the perps off each other. Most jerks, criminal or not, are insecure and highly egocentric. If you convince them that their real threat is within the ranks of their own crew, it can be surprisingly easy to get them off your back entirely.

Here's an example of what I mean. A couple of homeowners in a neighborhood facing a contentious city project were taking charge of the situation in a very annoying way. They were constantly calling and ringing the doorbells of all the neighbors, trying to get everyone as riled up as they were with conspiracy theories and plans for taking on city hall.

One of the bothered neighbors had the brilliant idea of taking on the terrible twosome with the old divide-and-conquer technique. We could tell each of them, he suggested, that the other's ideas make more sense, thus turning them against each other, and then their united—and very irritating front—would go up in smoke. Sure enough, when this strategy was put into play, the dynamic duo soon forgot they had neighbors to harass, so preoccupied were they with duking it out with each other.

Eventually, the pair did resurface, but, predictably, with much more reasonable ideas and much less vim and vigor. They were *much* easier to deal with this way, and all was well.

Another way to deal with a mass attack is to level the playing field by finding a way to interact with only one of the opposing team. Get them to appoint a leader or spokesperson, and then you can go one on one. Or recruit your own teammates. Find like-minded people with whom to defend or present your point of view, at work, in the PTA, etc.

The important trick is not to *feel* outnumbered, even when you are. Several crazy people don't equal the might of one sane person. So when you know you're in the right, center yourself, stay cool, and forge ahead. I find this particularly effective against power-in-numbers bureaucracies. I've been on the phone trying to deal with a health insurance company blunder, for instance, and had the customer (dis)service reps gang up on me. When the nonsense one rep was spewing didn't dissuade me, he put another rep on the line. When I still refused to say that two plus two equals five, they got a company stooge a little higher up the food chain onboard as well. They thought their mere numbers would override the illogic of their argument. Wrong. My persistence won out in the end: even if only to get me off their collected backs, they finally conceded that I was right.

If you find yourself up against a rafter of turkeys (and turkeys *are* known as a "rafter" when they all get together—Google it; I'm right), employ the divide-and-conquer strategy. Set them fighting with each other, if they have to fight with someone. And you can walk blithely away whistling "Life is okay in America."

If You Were Dr. Phil, You'd Be on TV

Don't Try to Change a Turkey

One of the hardest lessons to learn about difficult people is that if they ever do change (and that's a big "if"), it probably won't be as a result of anything you say or do. We'd all love to dish out "aha" moments to our friends and family, but that's not our job—it's Dr. Phil's. Or Dr. Laura's. Or God's. Or somebody else's, but not yours or mine. You might be a wiz at changing tires, lightbulbs, or credit cards, but changing a person—that's a tougher task.

The upside is that if you stop trying to flip that switch in someone else's brain, you can lose the frustration that is a big part of the scrooged experience.

Deciding to pass up the challenge of changing another person doesn't mean you don't care or you aren't bothered. It's just that changing that person is not in your job description. In fact, your stubborn, persistent attempts to change, improve, or enlighten will only move *you* into the difficult column—perhaps under the "Know-It-All Buttinski" subhead.

We all are on our own path in life—no matter how many inconsiderate skateboarders or off-leash pit bulls seem to be infringing on our own little lane. You might be on the path of being a nice, honest person, trying to be a good parent and responsible citizen, and maybe even hoping to leave some kind of positive mark on the world. That jerk pestering you on your path is simply on his own very different path—call it Difficult Street.

Maybe he will one day come to a crossroads where he will decide to turn on to a nicer thoroughfare. He might hope for such a lane change, or he might be oblivious to the fact that such options even exist. There's not much you can do about this. Trying to tell him or show him or take him by the hand and drag him onto a better path are tactics that don't have a high success rate.

Sure, if he asks you for directions or for help reading the map, you should lend your nice-person hand. If he asks. Or if you see him heading for a brick wall he can't see, by all means, point it out. But truly, restraint is called for here. Most of the time, throwing yourself into the middle of someone else's path will only get you trampled. It may even have unintended negative consequences. Because—speaking of consequences—part of a creep's path to change might be facing up to the havoc he wreaks. Sparing him that reality slows down that process.

If you are personally familiar with the path of arrogance, dishonesty, or intolerance that a scrooge is on, it can be mighty hard not to try to change, fix, or enlighten that person—right now! But you have a better chance of enlightening others by living in the light yourself. (This *is* your job description.) That means being a nice person, a helpful person, a generous person. You (of course) are sympathetic, empathetic, and willing to share your own experience. You might even occasionally get in there a bit and help another person see the way—but remember: only the other person can make the change.

Open-Heart Policy

Staying Connected to Difficult People

I knew a man, Grant, whose job was to fire people. These firings weren't downsizing layoffs but rather terminations for cause. The people he had to fire had been difficult in one way or another—dishonest, unable to meet performance standards, rude to clients and customers, impossible for coworkers to deal with, etc.

In other words, Grant dealt with scrooges all year long.

Grant's experience is highly useful because we may have to "fire" some such people in our lives, terminating our relationships when we've learned, through repeated warnings and probationary periods, that we simply have no other choice.

Grant told me that no matter how obvious it was that many of these people needed to be fired, actually doing so was still not easy. He knew that some of the people he fired were capable of much better behavior. Despite their flaws, he liked several of these employees very much. And whenever he thought of anyone being out of work, perhaps angry, demoralized, and struggling to make ends meet, he could not help but feel sad.

But Grant had also thought the situation through in a very wise way. Though he was the one who had fired these people, it remained clear to him that responsibility for any hardships they now faced was their own; it was their own actions, not his, that had created hard consequences for them.

Grant also developed a way of doing this most difficult part of his job that I think can be applied to many other situations we all face. Neem Karoli Baba once said: "Do what you have to do with another human being, but never put him out of your heart." When there is nothing left to be said or done, we can still concentrate on keeping the other person in our heart—if not in our daily life. This is a subtle but powerful distinction that helps maintain our own well-being while extending positive feeling and energy toward the other person.

Grant didn't allow himself to dehumanize the people he had to fire just to make his task easier. He simply saw them as fellow human beings who had slipped off track. He remained hopeful that they could and would turn their lives around.

Think of someone in your life you just can't stand. Rather than replay all your grievances against this person, relax, breathe, and try to quiet your thoughts. Open your heart by thinking of this person as someone who wasn't born with the traits that bother you so much but who acquired them in ways and for reasons you might not know. Try to extend compassion to this person.

The next step is *not* getting on the phone, inviting the scrooge over, and hiring him or marrying her. Keeping someone in your heart is an action that takes place in your mind and spirit. And while it soothes your mind and spirit, I believe that on some level it is also doing the other person some good. Not a bad day's work.

Watch and Learn from Mr. or Mrs. Ballistic

It Pays to Study Rude People

Mean people aren't all bad. I've found that they can serve a quite useful purpose. You can study jerks as though you were a med student performing an autopsy, or a CSI agent studying a crime scene. Bad behavior can be fascinating if you observe it with objectivity.

Years ago I was checking into a hotel in St. Louis, late at night, with my two sleepy girls in tow. An older business type trying to check in before me was well worth studying. He thought he had a reservation, but could not prove it. When this guy learned that the hotel not only was not holding a room for him but was overbooked, he just went ballistic. My girls and I took a couple of steps back and watched the show.

We were in an ideal classroom for studying how not to behave when frustrated. (I did feel for Mr. Ballistic; it was late, and he was clearly crankier than my kids.) The lesson learned? Do the exact opposite of what this guy did, point by point. Stay calm, attempt to establish rapport with the person who might be able to help you over the obstacle, and if you go over the head of this person, try to be even nicer to the supervisor, manager, or boss. Oh, and don't kick things. And don't swear.

As I pointed out to my girls, even if the hotel staffers had been able to find this guy a room, why would they give it to someone who had just spent twenty minutes proving he was unstable? Wouldn't it be logical for them to prefer to get him out of their establishment? Hotel staff routinely make amends for such booking errors or misunderstandings by finding the guest a room nearby and offering transportation and other freebies. Ballistic was not going to get a gift basket.

My girls learned quite a lesson that night. When it was our turn to check in, my youngest told the receptionist our confirmation number and then did something for which I'll always be proud: she told the clerk what a great job she had done with that "mean man." "I'm not sure what I would have done," my girl continued, "but you sure did great." The hotel worker told my daughter that her comments had made her night and that all the unpleasantness was worth it because she was able to meet such a sweet little girl. But wait, it gets better. Because we waited so patiently, the nice receptionist gave us coupons for a free breakfast.

So the next time you come across someone like Mr. Ballistic, slip into your forensics-lab role and put him or her under the microscope. Analyze and scrutinize with clinical objectivity. See what you can learn. You may not get a free breakfast out of your research, but I guarantee it will leave you feeling more detached, less scrooged, and maybe even like one of those cool crime unit agents on TV.

Hunt Hard for Something to Like

Nobody's Totally *Unlovable —*
Right?

My friend Bruce is a mediator who works with people and groups to help them negotiate solutions. If a particularly difficult person is present, the first thing he does is to try to lighten things up by finding some way to make that person laugh. Bruce, therefore, has a tough job. But when he succeeds, he is able to establish much-needed rapport with the potentially problematic person.

Bruce believes, and I think he's right, that difficult people are often self-centered. Their obnoxious behavior toward others is usually about themselves. In a roundabout way, they are reacting to perceived slights or threats to their own well-being.

Bruce recalls listening to a man whose coworkers all thought he was a total jerk. My friend let the guy talk and listened for something he could work with. After some small talk, Bruce realized that the jerk was a huge fan of the Green Bay Packers. So Bruce made a funny comment about the Packers having destroyed his team, the Forty-Niners. The jerk laughed, realized he had some common ground (or football field) with my friend, and the atmosphere in the room was instantly less tense.

Another technique is to look for something to like—or at least not hate. When we're around jerks, it's hard not to focus solely on what irks us—their tone of voice, their selfishness, their mean actions or manipulative words. But that is never all there is to see. It may require some effort, but make a mental shift, get out a magnifying glass if need be, and look until you find one little or big thing you can legitimately put in the plus column about this nut.

I'll give you a personal example. I was dealing with a woman whom I absolutely could not stand. (There. I said it.) I really (really) hated so much about her—she was loud, arrogant, and selfish. What was there to like? When I had to be in her company, all I could think was, "*Yuk. When will this be over?*"

As though to punish me, the gods of fate saw fit to put me in a situation that required prolonged contact with this woman, and a serious conflict ensued. I had nothing to lose, since I already felt like I was in a suburb of hell, so I remembered my own advice and tried it. Was there something I could find to like about this person?

It took a while (and it felt like forever), but I finally realized that this woman was remarkably articulate, even during heated debate. This is a rare and really quite admirable talent. So I admired it, and I even went so far as to compliment her on it. It's not like the rain stopped, the sun burst out, and the birds started to sing, but this little act did improve the climate in the room—tremendously. She softened, and so did I. Being sincere in my compliment somehow helped me dial down my dislike for her.

My "hunting trip" brought good results, and yours can, too. If you can lighten a tense situation, find common ground, or simply discover something positive about the jerk in question, you'll be rewarded with a new set of eyes with which to see him or her. You may be surprised at the new view.

Scheduling Your First Intervention

Confronting Difficult People as a Group

Unless you're stranded alone together on a desert island, you probably aren't the only person bothered by the scrooge who's getting under your skin. Chances are good that this person has a wrecking-ball relationship with a number of your mutual acquaintances.

You see this often in the workplace. The office irritant may be a gossip, someone who tries to get ahead by undermining others, or a long-winded time-waster in meetings who just loves the sound of his voice. This kind of scrooge annoys a whole group of people all at once. (Do he get bonus points for mass irritation?)

When a group of people are being scrooged by the same person, it's time to take group action. Intervention is a common tactic used with someone who has a problem with alcohol or drugs. It gives family members, coworkers, friends, and loved ones a chance to get together and share their concerns about the addict's behavior. A recovery-oriented intervention is a good model for group action toward a scrooge because, unlike that time in the fourth grade when you all made Melissa cry, this isn't about punishing, shaming, or ostracizing. The idea isn't to "gang up" on the person but to make it crystal clear that you are all aware of the problem behavior, that you are all being affected by it, and that you've all had it up to here. What do we want? Change! When do we want it? Now!

When a group gets serious about a problem and handles it properly, the chances that the person causing it will listen up are greatly enhanced.

Almost any kind of group (friends, coworkers, family members) can use this template. Get yourselves together and compare notes. Assemble your common complaints. Then plan a time to meet with the troublemaker.

When you meet, be honest but not mean. Letting everyone speak can have a powerful effect: the subject of the meeting can see that it isn't just one or two people blowing things out of proportion. It is critical to be specific and use examples but never to be drawn into rehashings of the events or actions in question. Everyone's tone should be serious (you do mean business), but devoid of anger and judgment. This is not an attack: you are simply stating the fact that certain behaviors are unacceptable.

It's common for the difficult person at the center of the intervention to become defensive and angry, justifying his or her behavior and making counter-accusations. This is totally understandable. No one likes to have the errors of their ways pointed out, and this tendency can be even more pronounced in difficult people precisely because of the personal issues, blind spots, and blockages that make them so annoying in the first place.

Interventions don't always work, but they often do. It's hard for a person to deny the perceptions of a whole group. If you begin to see improvements, applaud them. An intervention lets someone know that his or her behavior has been seen and judged unacceptable; it's only right to follow up by mentioning the positive changes you see. As those dealing with addicted loved ones well know, more than one intervention may be necessary. But there's strength, comfort, and support in numbers. So band together for the common good. By speaking with a collective voice, that annoying person just may realize that change is the best way back into healthy relationships.

Go Toe-to-Toe, and Heart-to-Heart

Clearing the Air

Sometimes the only way to deal with a scrooge is eyeball to eyeball. When your bottled-up anger or disappointment starts spilling over into day-to-day life, that's your cue to schedule some face time with that person you've been avoiding. But instead of going toe-to-toe, like boxers meeting in the ring before Round 1, try to go heart-to-heart. No need to turn this clear-the-air session into the Ultimate Fighting Championship.

The setup is straightforward. You and Mr. or Mrs. Scrooge simply agree to sit down together to discuss your differences in a respectful and cordial way. The goal is to put any unresolved issues on the table, then sweep them away together.

Although these types of sit-downs, like group interventions, can become confrontational, they can also be extremely healing. To succeed at clearing the air, you need to create a safe environment by establishing two basic rules ahead of time. Then you'll be amazed at how productive these little honesty-and-healing sessions can become.

The first rule to establish before anything is said is that you both will keep an open mind. This goes for us, too, not just the scrooge. We can't approach this self-righteously with the final verdict already in mind. Entrenched opinions and preconceptions (he's wrong, I'm right) will sabotage your bridge-building efforts. The goal of coming together is not ultimately about airing grievances, but fixing the problem, so do your best to let go of your assumptions. If things are so bad that it has come to a face-to-face meeting between the two of you, then an open mind is the first step to getting past this scrooge-sized roadblock.

The second rule is to make sure that the two of you take turns talking. While one is talking, the other must listen—no interrupting, no making faces, no looking for a quick getaway. Paying this kind of attention isn't easy, but it can become easier if you attempt to listen not just with your head but with your heart. A heart can intuit, feel sympathy, and otherwise see beyond words that sound illogical, mean, or mad. For example, if you tell me that you think I've gotten bigheaded and self-centered about my work, my heart might be able to detect beneath your anger your pain at my being less available for our friendship.

If listening is a challenge, try this exercise. When the scrooge is done speaking, briefly sum up what you've heard, giving him or her a chance to correct any misunderstandings right away.

This rule, and the first, may make you uncomfortable, but they are necessary. This is not a Take Session. That's another human being sitting across from you, even if all you see is a pain-inducing scrooge. Give him or her the same respect you want to receive.

During my adult lifetime I've had approximately half a dozen clearing-the-air sessions. I've asked for about half of them, and friends and family members have asked me for the other half. On two occasions I learned, quite to my surprise, that I was the person being the scrooge. I was able to see this because the others involved followed the rules and were so non-confrontational that I did not have a knee-jerk reaction to what they were saying. I remain grateful to these individuals to this day—even though I'm also a bit embarrassed and quite sorry—because they cared enough to initiate this exchange, which probably saved our relationships.

As every living, pink-hearted person knows, grudges and resentment usually get worse over time. So when the air between you becomes heavy with things unsaid, say them. And if you speak heart to heart, instead of going toe to toe, you have a chance to see eye to eye.

Size Up Your Opponent

Advice Before Round 1

You probably think you have that scrooge of yours all figured out, given how much time you spend thinking about him or her. But have you really sized up your scrooge? A featherweight never intentionally enters the ring with a heavyweight, and so you should avoid similar mismatches. Dealing with difficult people is like boxing, without the violence (one hopes) and without Don King (one hopes). Both boxing and scrooge-management require finesse and footwork. So ask yourself a few questions about your sparring partner before getting into the ring.

For instance, from your prior experience of this scrooge, does he or she tend to go all fifteen rounds in a given match? Is this person driven by the need to have the last word? Will this conflict drag on until both of you are bloodied and exhausted? You might need extra training for all those rounds.

More importantly, is he or she basically a reasonable person or a wild card who might fly off the handle once you initiate the bout? You might not want to take any chances with such a person. Perhaps you could avoid the fight and shift the battle to your own mind, where a few adjustments in attitude, meditation, visualization, etc. would win the day.

My friend Janet is smart and eloquent. You'd think (since I too am smart and eloquent!) that the two of us would be highly successful at talking out our differences and devising solutions. Au contraire. In her eloquence, Janet tends to write novel-length e-mails about issues. Then I write back. Then she writes back. Then I write, "I think we're done," only to have her agree but then summarize the whole darn thing in a way I just have to write back and correct—which only starts the whole e-mail train rolling down the tracks again.

Furthermore, Janet has a crazy-making tendency to say, "Never mind, you're right," but in a tone that lets you know she is patronizing you and doesn't really believe it for a second. I may sound like I'm describing a really difficult person, but in fact Janet has been a great friend of mine for a very long time. I love her. But I have had to conclude, in sizing her up, that discussing disputes is just not worth it.

We need to pick our battles carefully. Life doesn't give us time to fight every match, even if we think we could win them all. Given the number of difficult people in the world, and in your life, confronting them all could become a full-time job.

Here's an extreme example. Who hasn't had a gripe with a big company? But if visions of lawsuits dance through your head, think twice. No matter how right you are, you might not have the time or money to make your case through the courts. The company no doubt has a team of lawyers and publicity and public relations departments ready to go. I love a good underdog story as much as the next person, but it is okay to let someone else be that hero.

The smart decision might be figuring out if there's an opponent in your weight class who can correct the situation. For example, try dealing with a place of purchase rather than a manufacturer, or attempt to get satisfaction through customer service rather than legal channels. Perhaps you could "bulk up" fast by getting a consumer rights organization, or some other entity, to help you fight your battle.

In the end, it's not just a matter of sizing up your "opponent." Take measure of the offense—or offenses—as well. You don't need a mallet to squash an ant. As you consider this issue of proportion, why not sleep on it for a few nights? Slights can shrink as if by magic simply with the passing of a little time.

And last but not least, size yourself up. How much time and emotional energy are you willing to expend on the issue? Do you have more important things to worry about? If you've been tired or preoccupied recently, perhaps you're a little unsure about your ability to see a situation clearly. If so, you might regret any action you take right now. Are you so competitive that you can't imagine sitting out any contest? Take a break and see how that feels for a change.

Take a good long look at your "opponent," at yourself and at the situation before you enter the ring. If you're anything like me, you'll find that most fights aren't worth fighting. Why get your nose bent out of shape?

*

Acceptance

The Ultimate Solution

I may have hinted at the subject of this chapter in many of the previous chapters: it is one of the most fundamental lessons in learning to thrive in a world filled with scrooges and scroogettes. Here is the lesson: difficult people and difficult situations are unavoidable. Here's the advice: give up and get on with life.

Acceptance (once you get the hang of it) instantly frees you from the frustration associated with difficult people, no matter who they are, whether loved ones or total strangers, and no matter what form their offensiveness takes, whether it be meanness, rudeness, or selfishness.

Acceptance may sound like inaction, but when you try to practice it, you'll see that it is anything but doing nothing. It sometimes requires more effort than the complaining, confronting, or clamming up you would normally do. But I'm also happy to report that *with* practice—and once you experience the freedom it brings—acceptance can become almost second nature.

Most of us spend too much time wishing that people would be other than they are. From wishing the barista at the coffee shop would get some people skills first thing in the morning to wondering when the person we sleep with will stop commandeering the blankets in the middle of night, we need to accept that most people just aren't going to change.

Acceptance is made easier when you realize that the behavior that irritates you isn't aimed at you (even though you're the one who wakes up shivering in bed) or indulged in because of you (the barista doesn't dislike you per se). The behavior is just part of who the other person is—maybe not forever, but at least for right now. Accepting people's quirks or flaws doesn't just take changing them off your to-do list—it also gives you the time and energy to change the things you can.

Mark had been a top student in college and earned honors in graduate school as well. He had a prestigious job and seemed to excel at everything he attempted. Mark would probably have said that his greatest frustration in life was that his son was not a good student and showed no interest in higher education. His son simply was not interested in competing in the educational arena in which Mark had excelled.

Mark was hard on his son about this attitude toward school, leading the boy to feel unloved and not accepted for who he was. Mark felt scrooged by his son; his son felt scrooged by his father.

Mark was able to become less demanding when he was forced—after recognizing how futile his frustration was—to entertain the idea of just accepting his son as he was. No one expects cats to fly or lemon trees to sprout oranges, Mark realized, so he slowly stopped being so disappointed. Naturally, his son felt the shift.

I am not suggesting that we accept the unacceptable. But the next time you come face to face with mean or selfish people, try letting them be mean, selfish people. Maybe this cat will one day fly. (And I'm not convinced Mark's son will never go to college.) But apparently not today. That's the news. Accept it.

*

Terrible Teens
and Suggestions on
How to Tame Them

*Humble Advice from a Father of
Two (Mostly Wonderful) Teens*

For the record, I love teenagers. After all, I have two of my own who may glance at this book someday (dream on, Dad). But I also hear from *other* parents that while they certainly love their teenagers, they don't much *like* them—or their friends.

In the parents' perception, it was only yesterday that their kids looked up to them, respected them, and sought out their company and advice. Now, not so much. Okay, not at all. The parents feel scrooged and start to act from this place of frustration, becoming stricter or paranoid, yelling, showing a lack of trust, or even retreating in confusion. Then of course the kids feel scrooged and start acting out.

The teen years are a bit like the "terrible twos" plus a dozen or more years. The number of physical and psychological changes going on pretty much guarantees some bumps and bruises. But some of these can be avoided by you, the all-wise, all-caring Parent. You may not feel in charge any longer, but you have to take charge of guiding the relationship through until your teen's brain returns to planet Earth——or things will only get worse. After all, your teen is ill-equipped to manage the relationship at this point. And he or she has more important things to do, like hanging out at MySpace.com, trying to land a date, and racking up your cell phone bill.

Perhaps the most important thing in the world to a teen is to feel included. This is tricky to understand. On the one hand, teens want to be included in, say, a family. However, they also want to become completely independent. So sometimes, owing to this completely natural internal conflict, they send mixed messages and act in contradictory ways. One minute they may want you to tuck them in and tell them a story, and the next they're telling *you* a story and sneaking out of the house at night.

It's hard not to react with anger and worry if your kid does sneak out at night—going goodness knows where with God knows who. But extreme reactions tend to feel like rejection to teens. Yes, kids need boundaries, and on their good days they might even realize that you are freaking out because you care so much, but, well, teens don't have all that many good days.

So we adults have a tough role to play. We will always be a bit wrong in the eyes of our once adoring offspring. Give up that dream for now. Acceptance is your only avenue of success. Adoration may return later.

As mentioned, the need to feel included (in a group of friends, in a family) and the need to feel independent (they do have to grow and test their wings— unless you *want* them living at home at age twenty-seven) combine to create erratic behavior in your teen. This is therefore a time for you to practice the "pick your battles" principle. For instance, if you choose to not see your kid's tall tale as a sign of disrespect or manage not to react to it as though it were a harbinger of future corporate malfeasance, you can prevent the cycle of parent-child conflict escalation.

Suppose your seventeen-year-old son comes to you and tells you he's not going to spend Christmas with the family. This year, he announces, he's spending it with his girlfriend—his first love, the love of his life, the person he thinks he's going to marry.

Even though you are probably heartbroken and won't mention this desertion in your annual Christmas brag letter, remember your son's very real need at this point to differentiate himself from his family. Sadly, he also probably needs to experience his own first heartbreak not long after the love of his life leaves him well before Christmas. You need to let these things happen.

If you dig in your heels and refuse, you might have a sullen son at your Christmas celebration, plotting his New Year elopement with his Juliet. And he may stop sharing his feelings and choices with you altogether, which would be more than a drag.

I'd suggest that instead you tell him you are happy for him that he's found this swell girl (though you need not pretend to love her pierced lip). Let him know that you understand his desire to share the holiday with someone who is so important to him. Remind him that he's important to your family too, and ask if he can see a way to spend time with both groups. He'll feel loved, needed, included, and independent. And he'll be solving a dilemma and making a choice and a decision—all skills he needs to get good at if he's ever going to fly out of the nest.

Remember, I have teens of my own, so I know how very unpredictable, dramatic, and illogical relating with them can feel. What works for me might not for you, and what worked today might not tomorrow. But I do think that this is one instance where taking

the time to get inside the head of the person driving you nuts can really pay off. You can't walk away
from your teenagers, and you certainly don't want
them to, so you need all the insight and compassion
you can muster. This is your challenge, your job,
as the parent of a teen. The hours are long and the
work can feel thankless, but the payoffs down the
line will be worth it.

When the Boss
Ain't So Boss

*Changing the Script
to Solve Work Problems*

Most of us spend our time a) working, b) sleeping, c) doing other things we enjoy, in that order of time spent. The problem with this list is that a) working comes first, and that a) working generally entails having a boss. Even if you are your own boss, clients or crucial partners or customers can play the part of the boss in your life, looking over your shoulder, cramping your style, telling you how to do your job. Few people—perhaps only the Pope and whoever is currently ruling Uganda—have the luxury of a boss-free life. Even the president of the United States comes up for a quadrennial job performance review and possible firing.

I'm around a lot of people in my work, traveling and talking with hundreds a year, and one thing I've observed is that while many people complain about their boss, most bosses are pretty oblivious to what's being said about them. They generally feel great about their employees, think they have a good rapport with their underlings, and would, I'm sure, be mystified by the anger and resentment they often engender.

I think a large part of this situation is based on inappropriate role-playing, a routine you might come across with a variety of the turkeys in your life.

Many bosses consciously or unconsciously believe that they are supposed to be aloof, in charge, unwavering, nitpicking, and suspicious. They think this is part of the job description for The Boss.

By the same token, sometimes saying, "I hate my boss," is simply part of the role we play as employees.

No matter how qualified or talented your boss is, the position is really only that. Your boss isn't a boss; he or she is a man or woman in the role of boss. Just like that old advice to nervous public speakers—picture your audience in their underwear—thinking of your boss as a person playing a role can help you understand his or her actions and feel less affected by them.

This strategy can be utilized by either the boss or the employee. The boss could recognize that he actually feels a bit trapped by what he thinks are the rules of his role. Perhaps he's a people person who prefers gathering differing opinions and working toward consensus. Maybe he's growing an ulcer, developing high blood pressure, and flirting with heart disease by trying to be harsh, decisive, and a little ruthless.

Or maybe you have a boss who misses the feeling of being part of the team, which seemed to disappear when she became captain. Recognizing this, she could work on changing the culture in her workplace—for instance, by putting changes in place that minimize a sense of hierarchy.

If these scenarios seem as unlikely as another George Foreman boxing comeback, you, as an employee, can try shifting your perspective. Think of your boss as an actor in a role. How's he doing? Does the costume fit? Is he flubbing his lines? Think of him as someone who might have stage fright and regularly feels insecure—a feeling that causes him to act in defensive ways to cover it up. What does the audience (all you employees) think? Will his performance get a good review or a bad one? (Most bosses have bosses themselves.)

If your boss is not just your boss but also, essentially, a man or woman in a costume and on a stage while at work, can you cut him or her a bit more slack? For instance, do you, in your own work role and nine-to-five costume, ever feel the need to behave in slightly weird ways? Say, by waxing enthusiastic about a dumb idea, growing fond of an annoying client, or being really, really impressed with the receptionist's new haircut so that you can later ask him to screen a call?

I hope it goes without saying that I'm talking here about trying to understand your boss and learning to ride out relatively minor instances of irritating statements or behaviors. I'm not suggesting that you stay in a job that makes you miserable or that you learn to take pity on someone who's abusive, cruel, or unethical.

If your boss drives you batty but you like the job enough to stay, try viewing yourself and your boss as actors in a play. You aren't really your character, and neither is your boss—but you play them at work. Try changing the script in little ways that might have a big impact. It's worth a try, because every morning the curtain goes up and the act goes on and, somehow, work gets done. Break a leg.

Spin That Turkey

Is Their Behavior Irritating — or Charming?

Let's kvetch just a little about other people's habits, tics, and quirks. These traits can be endearing, like the way Grandma washes and re-uses the Chinette or your son blurts out embarrassing details of your home life in front of the neighbors. But habits, tics, and quirks are also like a day in the sun: too much exposure and they become major annoyances. If you are having a bad day, a little irritant can bore into your head like a power drill, leaving you begging for relief from the (capital A) Annoying person with whom you find yourself sharing the holidays, or a cubicle, or a bed, or a life.

Let's take a lesson from that person with the most thankless of jobs: the president's press secretary. No matter who's in that job, or who's in the Oval Office, this person spends the day spinning the news. Everything of importance that happens on the world stage gets recharacterized by this person in a way that's favorable to the president. Celebrities, too, have their own spinmeisters, those managers or "handlers" who explain why the young starlet was caught canoodling with a hipster who is not her husband, or how the leading man's recent arrest for "illegal solicitation" was really an attempt to show kindness to America's persistent underclass, and why isn't Congress doing more about poverty anyway?

Exercising your creative ability to spin your own life's minor annoyances can work wonders. Your turkey doesn't stop being a turkey, but you now find this person's idiosyncrasies interesting, or you realize how funny they are, or you cease to notice them altogether. While you are putting a new spin on the old, irritating quirk, you are distracted and taken out of the heat of the moment. And just like a politician, after spinning it for a while, you may eventually come to believe your own spin. (You weren't being bribed; you were listening to your constituents!)

Simply put, spinning is recharacterizing someone's behavior and looking at it differently—in a way that bugs you less. Look at the following examples and then think about where you could apply the principle in your own life.

I'm a little obsessive about being on time—so much so that a few people (actually more than a few) think it makes *me* irritating. (They need to learn to spin.) I get a little uptight when I'm running late, and to some people, particularly my kids, I'm really very neurotic about this.

I have a friend who has the opposite issue: Phil is habitually late. This habit of his used to drive me nuts, and I felt scrooged. While being kept waiting, my feelings would escalate, and though I found playful and finally serious ways of letting him know I was irritated, his behavior did not change.

I wanted to stay friends with Phil but couldn't see a way to avoid making our meetings (which he'd be late for) less stressful. So I found a way to make my waiting time work for me. Whenever I had a date with Phil, I also made a date with the book I was reading or the periodical I'd been meaning to get around to. I no longer had exasperating waiting time; I had a moment to myself, a break in the action, and some hard-to-find reading time. I actually began to look forward to my friend being a few minutes late.

I used to also feel shafted by the self-centeredness of others. Did they really not care about my life? Who did they think they were? Why did they think that play-by-plays about their day, week, or year were of interest to me?

I was once in a group of people and became aware of a me-me-me type. When other people described an experience or told a story, Mr. Me had to top it. His life was happier or sadder or more dramatic; it was just plain more important. Seeming to suffer through everyone else's words, he could barely hide his need to get back in the spotlight and talk about himself.

Given this "opportunity," I decided to perform an experiment. I spun my being subjected to Mr. Me as a chance to make him my subject. I wanted to learn all that I could about this subject, and so I drew him out further (that wasn't too hard), asking him questions, not in a cynical or mocking way but out of my new, genuine curiosity about what made this type of person tick. I learned about his hobbies, his relationship history, his aches and pains. I heard about people I didn't know and places I'd never been. It was actually kind of interesting once I decided I had a reason to care.

When you have to be around someone self-centered (Mr. Me) or find yourself waiting for the chronically tardy (late Phil), why not make the best of it with a little spin? My father did this when he was in the army and had a stereotypically brutal drill sergeant. Instead of griping with the other grunts about what a monster this guy was, my father decided to see him as his helper in getting into the best physical shape of his life. This scrooge went from dreaded drill sergeant to helpful personal trainer in one quick spin.

When a person is causing us more serious pain or inconvenience, spinning is not the way to go. We shouldn't deny cruelty, manipulation, or other forms of abuse. But there are plenty of times when playing the part of the press secretary will save you some serious stress. Turn on the spin cycle and recharacterize the quirky little habits you can't control. (For example: "No, I'm not dreading having Aunt Eunice's fruitcake again this year. It will bring back twenty years of fond memories.")

Check Your Mood at the Door

Size Up Your Emotional State Before Meeting a Scrooge

I've spoken and written a great deal about moods—how they can deceive us into thinking our life and our relationships are far worse than they really are. Never, however, is a basic understanding of moods more critical than when you're confronted with difficult people.

Here's a crash course on moods. When you're in a good mood, life looks pretty fabulous. You have perspective and some optimism. You feel warmly toward the people in your life—faults and all. Your career looks promising and satisfying to you, even if it's not your dream career. When you think about your future, you can see things improving. Likewise, when you think of your past, although it wasn't perfect, you've made peace with it. You have hope.

Bad moods are quite the opposite. When you're feeling down, life looks pretty difficult and bleak. Your relationships seem troubled, and even your favorite

149

*

people in the world—your kids, your spouse, your best friend—can sometimes seem like a burden. In a bad mood, you have virtually no perspective, and everything looks like an emergency. When you think of your career, the words that come to mind are "boring" and "dead end." When you think of your past, you feel like a victim, and when you think of the future, it doesn't look very promising.

For the sake of argument, let's assume that the difficult are not as changeable as your moods. The rude are always rude, the mean always mean.

If you think about or spend time around a mean person when you are in a bad mood, boom! It's a horrible combination. You are more vulnerable, everything is more dire, Ms. Mean is desperately annoying ... life stinks.

But if you are in a good mood, the odds are high that Ms. Mean will have a much milder, more insignificant effect on you. You might not notice her behavior, you might not care, or you might even feel sorry for someone who is so unpleasant.

Good moods also tend to leave us feeling "in the zone." Depending on your beliefs, being in the zone can make you feel guided by God, in touch with a higher power, intuitive, or as though you're channeling the wisdom of the universe. You are basically your best self, and from this place you feel able, without a lot of thought or deliberation, to say and do the right thing in a given circumstance. Being in the zone makes difficult people and situations much less ... difficult.

The lesson here is quite simple. Before meeting with someone you know to be difficult, check in on your own mood. If you're feeling down, find a way around or out of the encounter. If you can't do this, at least factor your mood into the equation, realizing in advance that you might be more sensitive, susceptible, or hair-trigger. Don't expect much of yourself in a bad mood, and try not to initiate or react. If you find yourself feeling "triggered," try to mentally step out of the situation for a moment and check on your mood again.

Most of us cycle through good, neutral, not-so-hot, and lousy moods all the time—sometimes in the space of a single day. Becoming aware of them and how they alter our perceptions can prevent a bad mood from turning into a bad scene. So pretend you have one of those great old mood rings, glance at it regularly, and act—or don't act—accordingly.

How NOT to Ruin Relationships with E-mail

Think Before You Send

E-mail is a terrific tool that can save you time, keep you in touch with friends and family—and ruin your relationships. It all depends on how you use it. Because e-mail is such a quick and easy way to share and gather information you'd think it would also be a no-fuss and relatively risk-free way of dealing with turkeys (or at least those turkeys who've been trained to use a computer). After all, you can organize and rewrite your thoughts, and you don' t have to risk getting flustered in a face-to-face encounter. You also get to have your say without listening to immediate reactions; you just click Send and you' re done. Easy.

But I've found that e-mail doesn't always work this way and may not be the path of least resistance when dealing with the difficult.

However technologically sophisticated it is, e-mail simply isn't subtle enough to convey the range of your feelings when you are angry or disappointed or when you're discussing a disagreement. It is simply too easy for your written words to be misinterpreted. Without the look on your face or the tone in your voice, and without the body language that accompanies actual conversation, your words can sound angrier than you intend, less serious, or too blunt.

Moreover, when one of your e-mails is misunder-stood, you're likely to get a note back taking you to task. This can go on and on—and on.

Mary was a little intimidated by her friend Sue. Sue was really good with words, liked nothing more than a good heated debate, and tended to dominate every conversation she was in. So when Mary had a gripe with her friend, she decided to confront her with an e-mail. She thought through her feelings and took a great deal of time composing the e-mail. After she sent it, she felt satisfied that she had been able to fully explain herself.

When Mary got Sue's reply, however, it seemed to her that Sue had read a different e-mail. It took Mary a lot of time to correct Sue's misconceptions—and she wound up having new gripes with her friend because of things Sue wrote in response to things she'd perceived in Mary's e-mail but that Mary hadn't intended. Ultimately, Mary had to do the very thing she'd been trying to avoid: pick up the phone and talk through the original situation.

A possible exception to my "no e-mail" rule is when two people try to talk and wind up polarized, in opposing corners. An apology in a brief e-mail can set the stage for a fresh conversation.

But conversation really is the best way to, well, converse, so cut to the chase and when you want to talk, talk.

Enough About You, Let's Talk About Me

The Arrogant of the Species

"Ghe thinks she knows everything." "He doesn't really listen; he just tells you what to do." "No matter what I say, she's already been there and done that." These are the kinds of comments I hear after people encounter an especially difficult personality trait—the kind that makes us scream, "Scrooge!" I'm talking about the arrogant of the species, and you don't need to travel far to discover them. These are the people who claim that they had a better vacation than you, that their kid is more popular than yours, and that they would never be in your predicament because they're too smart.

They're in line for God's job when He retires.

The person I'm thinking of when I write these words starts every conversation with a list of everything she has recently accomplished (a bit like one of those Christmas brag letters). Her litany of achievement is almost like a dare.

But as annoyed as people get about arrogance, it's actually one of the easiest scrooge behaviors to beat.

Have you ever been in a warehouse store and been slightly frustrated by the service—or more precisely, the lack of service? But if you stop and do the math—while wandering around searching for someone, anyone, who can answer your question—you might become less annoyed. You shop at this store for the low prices, and one way to keep prices low is to keep overhead low by hiring a small staff. Once you get it, you can stop focusing on the poor service and just enjoy the low prices. All it takes is a simple shift in your understanding.

You can have the same type of instant insight and corresponding change of feelings about an arrogant person by understanding where arrogant behavior comes from. Arrogant people work hard to inflate their accomplishments and puff up their lives because more often than not they have low self-esteem. They strut and brag and swagger because they are always concerned about what other people think of them. They don't *feel* worthy, so they have to make it a 24/7 effort to sell you (and themselves) on their worthiness.

The last time I saw the woman I just described, I thought about this. When she launched into her self-indulgent, self-aggrandizing speech, I was immune to irritation. She didn't shift—that's for sure—but I did. I knew that she needed to do what she was doing because she suffered from insecurity. How mad could I be at someone who was suffering?

When I run into arrogant people now, I simply let them go on and wait for them to finish. I usually say something polite, as if to agree with them about how wonderful they are. The way I think about it, this approach might help them to feel better about themselves. And if they feel better about themselves, they might stop being scrooges in the first place.

This strategy works 100 percent of the time with the braggarts, but it's more challenging to use with those sardonic scrooges who like to sprinkle their boasts with insults. Nevertheless, this same approach can work even with put-down artists. Obviously, there are limits to how many insults you can absorb, and by no means am I suggesting that you just grin and bear it. But this rude and selfish behavior comes from a weak and insecure place, and recognizing this fact can help defuse the insults. I urge you to give it a try. When that turkey waddles up and starts gobbling on about his or her latest accomplishments, you won't feel scrooged as much as amused.

Your Life
Is Your Message

People Notice How You Live,
Not What You Say

One of my very favorite sayings comes from Mahatma Gandhi: "My life is my message." When you get right down to it, that's really all we have to offer—our actions, our values, the way we live, our responses to adversity.

This saying is particularly pertinent when we're dealing with difficult people because, as we know, they are almost always a huge test of our own character. What I've found is that if I can manage to keep Gandhi's thought in mind when I'm face to face with a character-tester, I behave very differently than I do if I have only my own thoughts to keep me company.

I once hired a person to come and do some work on our home. He was going to do some odds and ends and be there the entire day. We scheduled the work weeks ahead of the actual day. I confirmed the appointment a few days in advance and then scheduled my entire day around his visit. When he arrived, he seemed like a really nice guy, and I anticipated the best. But about thirty minutes later, he walked into my home office and told me he was leaving because he had a "more important job" to attend to.

My initial reaction was a not very Gandhi-like fury. How dare he shun me for another job? What could be more important than my stuck doors and leaking windows? But then I remembered: "My life is my message." If I acted like an arrogant jerk, I'd be, well, an arrogant jerk. Did I want to be the kind of person who, when things did not go his way, sulked, got angry, and assumed he was being slighted? Nope. Did I want this apparently nice person to think of me as a hothead? Again, no. Did I want to burn my bridges and find a new handyman? Definitely not.

As I slowed down enough to remember Gandhi's wisdom, I also realized that I didn't know what "a more important job" meant. It could have been an emergency, an arrogant jerk (someone completely un-like me) breathing down his neck, or maybe a really high-paying offer that he simply couldn't pass up. Who knows? Not me. And it really didn't matter. It was what it was.

And since I am what I am—an average person try-ing to be a good person—I told the handyman, "I hope everything goes all right, and please call me when you get an opening." I could tell he was relieved that I didn't blow up at him, and you know what? He called me a few days later to reschedule. He then did the work really well and at a reasonable price. No harm done.

You virtually never offend another person or make matters worse when you pause to consider the ramifications of your words and actions. And instead of feeling scrooged or acting like one yourself, you can feel proud of your grace and equanimity.

Your life really is your message. What type of message are you sending?

Red Light Means "Relax"

Take a Breathing Break

Like many of my fellow California drivers, I used to get annoyed when I "missed" a light. I concocted elaborate schemes for getting even with the guy who (how dare he?) was only going the speed limit in front of me and left me hanging back at the red light. It's not like I was rushing my in-labor wife to the hospital; this was just my daily driving MO.

Then I heard the brilliant Buddhist monk Thich Nhat Hanh say that he loved red lights and stalled traffic because they gave him the chance to breathe deeply and be grateful.

Grateful? For traffic and red lights? It has taken me a while to get it, but what I *think* he's suggesting is that we should be grateful for a break in the action, a time-out for ourselves, and the opportunity to regain a sense of grounded calm in the midst of our dashing around.

I've since discovered that lots of busy people have devised a similar habit. Whether they're driving up to stop signs or red lights, being put on hold on the phone, or finding themselves on an elevator that is stopping at every floor, these people have decided that slowdowns are prompts for them to momentarily step out of their hectic day and back into themselves. Breathing slowly and deeply is the perfect way to do this. Instead of cursing the cosmos for throwing these everyday roadblocks in your path, you can thank fate for the much-needed pauses.

I've come to use some of the difficult people I deal with regularly as this kind of prompt. (Don't tell them.) When I see them coming or know I'm headed their way, I take a breathing break. I've even done this in their presence, and the great thing about breathing is that they just thought I was breathing.

When you take a few slow, deep, belly-expanding breaths, your shoulders relax, your thoughts mellow out, and, if you're anything like me, you often also get a hit of well-being. This is a great state to be in when dealing with the difficult. So great that you might actually find yourself looking forward to unwelcome encounters, red lights, and traffic jams. Well, let's not get carried away.

Discovering Your
Inner Turkey

Take Your Own Advice

As I end this book, I'm going to turn the microscope on myself, and I ask you to do the same. Friend, let's be real: deep inside of each of us lives an inner turkey. We've been exploring how we, the kind-hearted, considerate, gentle people of the planet, can live our lives in a world full of *them*—the obnoxious, incompetent, arrogant, and downright mean-spirited turkeys, scrooges, and jerks. But as I'm sure you've noticed by now, the enemy is often us. I believe it's far more productive to look at our own thoughts and actions than it is to concentrate on theirs. They grab enough of our attention as it is, don't you think?

I believe I'm a good person, and I try to do the best I can each day. My guess is that you do the same. But as I've been writing about all the ways in which we can feel scrooged by other people, I've bumped into a not-so-fun fact: I've got at least a tiny bit of virtually every bad trait I've described. Some of my friends, family, and business associates might even say more than a tiny bit. (I'll be buying them especially lavish gifts this Christmas.)

I know that I've hurt people's feelings, said and done the wrong thing at the wrong time, made countless mistakes, used poor judgment, driven poorly, and acted selfishly. In fact, I could go on and on. Recently, my sixteen-year-old daughter said to me, "Dad, you haven't made any serious mistakes since early this morning." It was lunchtime.

If the only people interviewed by my biographer were the buddy I badmouthed, the boss I didn't give my best to, and the friend whose calls I can't seem to return, I'd come across as the king of the scrooges.

So regardless of who we are, and no matter how hard we try, I think we are all a mixed bag, a smorgasbord of things we like, things we tolerate, and things we wish would go away. Our "tuna casserole" traits and "fruit cocktail in gelatin" characteristics don't make us bad people; they make us human. As Zorba the Greek put it, "I'm the whole catastrophe."

One of the reasons it's important to look in the mirror and face our own shortcomings is that, when we do this, it becomes pretty simple to give other people a break. When someone in your life is being difficult, that person too is just being human. You may wish he or she would go away and show their humanity to someone else, but, well, that's life.

The other payoff in cutting others some slack is our own freedom—freedom from feeling so very scrooged, freedom from hurt feelings or a brain clogged with revenge fantasies, freedom to move on and enjoy the filet mignon and garlic mashed potatoes, to focus on the nicer things on offer at the buffet of life.

As I've said several times throughout this book, not being irritated is not the same as failing to act when it's necessary or important. I'm not excusing negative or destructive behavior in any way whatsoever, and I'm not suggesting that you excuse it either. Instead, I'm suggesting that you mull over the strategies described in this book as you continue to try to stand up for what is right and avoid bad behavior. As you do, I believe that place of peace and inner tranquillity will enlarge in your life.

Fellow turkeys, how do we thrive in a world full of obnoxious, incompetent, arrogant, and downright mean-spirited people—in other words, people who, on occasion, act just like we do? By forgiving those traits in ourselves as well as in every other all-too-human person we meet along the way.

Don't Sweat It

100 Best Inspirations from
DON'T SWEAT THE SMALL STUFF

For the first time, the best of the best from the classic book that has reached almost 10 million readers.